Systematic Mythology

Systematic Mythology

Imagining the Invisible

Jennifer Agee

WIPF & STOCK · Eugene, Oregon

SYSTEMATIC MYTHOLOGY
Imagining the Invisible

Copyright © 2018 Jennifer Agee. All rights reserved. Except for brief quotations in critical publications or reviews, no part of this book may be reproduced in any manner without prior written permission from the publisher. Write: Permissions, Wipf and Stock Publishers, 199 W. 8th Ave., Suite 3, Eugene, OR 97401.

Wipf & Stock
An Imprint of Wipf and Stock Publishers
199 W. 8th Ave., Suite 3
Eugene, OR 97401

www.wipfandstock.com

PAPERBACK ISBN: 978-1-5326-4816-8
HARDCOVER ISBN: 978-1-5326-4817-5
EBOOK ISBN: 978-1-5326-4818-2

Unless otherwise noted, all scripture quotations are from the New Revised Standard Version Bible, copyright © 1989 National Council of the Churches of Christ in the United States of America. Used by permission. All rights reserved worldwide.

The masculine pronoun for God is kept unchanged in quoted material.

"And All the Tribes Fear Him" was originally published in *Currents in Theology and Mission*, Volume 41, Number 1. Used by permission. The photo of a model totem pole is used by permission from Cornelia Duryée and the Seattle Art Museum.

"Vigil" and "Picture Perfect" were first published on *Transpositions* (transpositions.co.uk), the online journal for the Institute for Theology, Imagination and the Arts at the University of St Andrews.
Used by permission.

Manufactured in the U.S.A.

for my god

Every scribe who has been trained for the kingdom of heaven is like the master of a household who brings out of his treasure what is new and what is old.

—Matthew 13:52

Among the many and varied literary and artistic studies upon which the natural talents of man are nourished, I think that those above all should be embraced and pursued with the most loving care which have to do with things that are very beautiful and very worthy of knowledge.... And since a property of all good arts is to draw the mind of man away from the vices and direct it to better things, these arts can do that more plentifully, over and above the unbelievable pleasure of mind (which they furnish).

—Copernicus, *De Revolutionibus Orbium Coelestium (On the Revolutions of the Heavenly Spheres)*

Even the most imperfect knowledge of something worth knowing is more to be striven after than the most certain knowledge of something inconsequential.

—Aristotle, quoted by Eberhard Jüngel, *God as the Mystery of the World*

In the Scriptures we are in our Father's house where the children are permitted to play.

—Raymond Brown, *The Sensus Plenior of Sacred Scripture,* quoted by Walter Brueggemann, *An Introduction to the Old Testament*

I was constantly seeing, and on the outlook to see, strange analogies, not only between the facts of different sciences of the same order, or between physical and metaphysical facts, but between physical hypotheses and suggestions glimmering out of the metaphysical dreams into which I was in the habit of falling. I was at the same time much given to a premature indulgence of the impulse to turn hypothesis into theory.

—George MacDonald, *Lilith*

Θεὸν οὐδεὶς ἑώρακεν πώποτε· μονογενὴς θεὸς ὁ ὢν εἰς τὸν κόλπον τοῦ πατρὸς ἐκεῖνος ἐξηγήσατο.

No one has ever seen God; the only Son, who is in the bosom of the Father, he has made him known.

—John 1:18 [RSV]

Τίνος ἡ εἰκὼν αὕτη καὶ ἡ ἐπιγραφή;

Whose image and inscription is this?

—Matthew 22:20

Contents

Acknowledgments | xi

1 **Seen and Unseen** | 1
  Prolegomena   1
  The Systematic Approach   3

2 **What Is a Myth?** | 8
  A Modern Difficulty   10
  A Working Definition   16

3 **Significance** | 19
  Ultimate Concern   21
  Anxiety and Art   24
  Heroes versus Mortals   28
  Live Wire   30
  Informed Substance   31

4 **Imagination** | 36
  Poetry   37
  Giving Form to Thought   39
  The Invisible God   41
  Making Images   44
  Planning or Devising   49

Contents

5 **Mythopoesis** | 52
　The Stories We Live By　52
　The Exegetical Imagination　56
　Sacred Texts　62

6 **Systematic Mythology** | 69
　Caveats: Where Mythology Fails　72
　Myth versus Materialism　75
　Living Myth　76
　Enacted Exegesis　78
　The Author of All Our Story　82
　The Crucified God　84
　Practice　85
　Conclusion　87

Afterword: A Blessing | 90

Appendices: Applied Mythology
And All the Tribes Fear Him | 91
Iceland, January 2010: A Mythic Meditation | 102
Advent | 108
Vigil | 110
Picture Perfect | 111
A Night at the Salt Kiln | 114

Bibliography | 117
Subject Index | 121
Scripture Index | 125

Acknowledgments

THIS BOOK BEGAN AS my MA thesis at Wartburg Theological Seminary. Sam Giere was my advisor; Duane Priebe was my reader and mentor; and Dan Olson offered essential reading suggestions. Paul Schick, Øystein Aronsen, and Garrett Siemsen participated in our collegial thesis seminar.

John Hobbins, Kirstin Jeffrey Johnson, Paul Wallace, and Ben Dobyns read the manuscript and offered important suggestions and support.

Bill Holm, Charles Mudede, and Renee Splichal Larson each helped in unique ways.

My parents, Chuck and Candi Thonney, provided a firm and loving foundation.

Matthew Agee and Jane Agee were essential in every way.

Thank you all.

1

Seen and Unseen

Prolegomena

MANY YEARS AGO I was sitting in a dive bar on Capitol Hill in Seattle, enjoying a conversation with a friend. Someone else joined us and shoehorned his way into our philosophical musings. Inevitably, religion came up.

"Feh!" the newcomer scoffed. "Who wants to sit on a cloud playing a harp for all eternity, anyway?"

I stiffened. I knew my friend was an atheist. He was also an accomplished writer and thinker. In contrast, I was fresh out of college, still reeling from the body blows my precritical faith had taken there. I felt ill-prepared to exercise my apologetics muscles in the present company, but I had no choice. Reluctantly, I began to gather my thoughts.

But to my surprise, there was no need. My friend leaned over and murmured, almost confidentially: "If there is anything after death, it *must* be a lot more interesting than that. A genuine argument requires imagination."

I grew up among the Plymouth Brethren, a faithful group of Christians who gave me a rock-solid biblical foundation together with a precritical, literal, intensely Christocentric hermeneutic. One of my early passions was reading mythology and speculative fiction (fantasy). As an unabashed re-reader of my favorite books, I practically memorized the works of C.S. Lewis and J.R.R. Tolkien. I developed a working knowledge of Greek and Norse mythology in particular, and an acquaintance with many other traditions.

After college I became interested in science, especially theoretical physics. I wanted to learn as much about the cosmos as possible. What was the world made of, and could I still believe in God after hearing out science's case for reality? If God didn't create the world in seven days, as I had been taught, what did that mean for the reliability of Scripture? I was pursuing God among quasars and quantum uncertainty—testing the boundaries of my beliefs in an effort to deepen my faith. And that faith remained: trust in, love for, and commitment to God as revealed in Jesus Christ. The more I learned, the more wonderful creation became.

A decade later I attended Wartburg Theological Seminary, where I was introduced to historical criticism as well as systematic theology. I experienced the latter discipline as a homecoming. Although the creeds were new to me, the systematization of life and "talk about God"[1] was my native mode of thought.

Historical criticism was another matter. It seemed to deconstruct everything in Scripture I still assumed was sacred, even as it offered useful interpretive tools, such as genre and narrative criticism. How should this new information be incorporated? What does postcritical truth look like?

There was also the recurring question of pluralism: of other cultures, of other gods. What is mythology, and what (if anything) is it good for? If I continue to insist on reading (and re-reading) my favorite fiction, what (if any) is its value? Finally, I wondered, is there such a thing as Christian mythology? If so, is it "truer" than other kinds? How is it related to theology—another, more "rational" form of talk about God?

---

1. Talk about God (theology) versus stories about God (mythology).

The Systematic Approach

Systematic theology. Systematic theology is a fundamental discipline that extracts the ideas behind the stories that have been handed down to us in Scripture and articulates them in a rational, logical system.[2] Systematic theology puts orthodox Christian belief in conversation with modern knowledge and culture, including the sciences. Its goal is a comprehensive, logical explanation of the world, our place in the world, and what and who we mean when we say "God" or "Jesus Christ." What (that is, who) is the Trinity? What is sin? What is redemption? Why and how did God create the cosmos? What will be the conclusion of it all?

Systematic theology is summarized in the creeds—concise, logical rules that form the basic structure and limits of orthodoxy. The creeds have been deduced from Scripture and vigorously tested in the crucible of human religious history. (They have also been aptly described as a form of protection for the masses against the theorizing of the overeducated.[3])

Again, systematic theology is the rational articulation of Christian faith in light of the Scriptural witness, ordered by the creeds, in conversation with neighbors. It faithfully confesses orthodox, traditional Christian belief, interpreting it anew for each new generation. It is the "creative interpretation of existence," and it deals with "the meaning of being for us."[4]

Like any logic puzzle, the rules of orthodoxy are complex and can be enjoyable. Theology is beautiful, useful for regulating thought and avoiding error, and pleasurable in its own right as a field of study. A systematic theology of two or three dense volumes is an impressive accomplishment from its author and (if we can understand it) may lead us to believe we have made headway

---

2. Thomas Cahill defines a theologian as "someone who can articulate clearly the intellectual affirmations that lie behind the stories." Cahill, *Desire of the Everlasting Hills*, 122.

3. "[T]he great orthodox creeds are the ordinary Christian's protection against the ingenuity of the wise and intellectually superior." McDermott, "Evangelicals Divided," para. 36.

4. Tillich, *Systematic Theology*, 3–4, 22.

toward comprehending Truth. But there are at least two problems with this. First, God is anything but comprehensible by God's creatures.[5] And second, few or none of us inhabit a purely rational world of logical rules and ideas.

Although rules, systems, and logic can be delightful topics for heady study, most of us spend most of our time in the dust: in the body, in the things that are visible, corporeal, experienced. To speak in Platonic or idealist terms, this is concept versus thing; idea versus image; mind versus body; rational versus irrational; *theology versus mythology*.

"In the language of rationalism of the nineteenth century, the term 'myth' indicated what is not contained in reality, *the product of the imagination* (Wundt), or *what is irrational* (Levy-Bruhl)."[6]

A human individual is not reducible to lists of principles. Nor is a human culture. We are embodied; and we tell stories. True, stories often have an inner logic or grammar that includes elements such as setting, characters, plot, and narrative coherence.[7] Yet, they are fundamentally different from a rational system of ideals such as mathematics or philosophy. What is rational is based on reason, deduction, logic. Narratives are not founded on pure reason, but on imagery; they re-present events or impressions to the senses, and they do so in a way that is interpretive, that creates meaning. A story is as different from a principle as Monet's paintings of water lilies are different from the formula $E=mc^2$, although both are accurate descriptions of light. In this sense, stories are not rational; they are ir-rational or imaginative. Mythology is less like a set of concepts or

---

5. "Comprehension" can also imply mastery, as in John 1:5. When comprehension seeks to control, it becomes the fundamental sin of idolatry.

6. Emphasis mine. John Paul II, *Man and Woman,* 138n4. "Irrational" in this context simply means not founded on rationality or logic. The footnote goes on to explain that "the twentieth century has modified the concept of myth" and to describe concisely several of the major myth theories and theorists. We now join this conversation as postmoderns in a positivistic world where the church is learning to take up and revivify ancient practices, engage with modern culture, and as always, proclaim the kerygma.

7. McAdams, *Stories We Live By,* 25; Kelley, *Grief,* 80–82.

rules, and more like a picture. It's not thought out or deduced, but experienced (although maybe analyzed afterward).

Now, following the definition of systematic theology above, we can say that systematic mythology is the *imaginative* articulation of Christian belief in conversation with Scripture, tradition, and modern culture. An "imaginative articulation" is a narrative—a myth (μῦθος, *mythos*).

Visible and invisible. "We believe in one God, the Father, the Almighty, maker of heaven and earth, of all that is, seen and unseen." This first confession of the Niceno-Constantinopolitan creed reminds us that Christian tradition considers created reality to be composed of what is "seen" and "unseen" (or "visible" and "invisible").[8] The "invisible" is often taken to mean powers and authorities, such as angels or cosmic rulers.[9] However, in terms of the persistent Western dichotomy of science and poetry, we can also equate what is "invisible" with the mind, with ideas, with the Logos, the Paradigm, or with binary information,[10] the fundamental laws of physics—and with systematic theology, especially when it is "pursued and presented in highly syllogistic and logical form, as pared of imagery as possible."[11]

Science and modern computing technology have unveiled the nature of information at a popular level.[12] We have cracked the code of DNA, which dictates the executable form for every living thing via a "language" of just four chemical symbols. Chemical reactions, atomic values, and the laws of physics—all expressible in figures

---

8. Colossians 1:15–16; Romans 1:20; Hebrews 11:3. See also Genesis 1:2 LXX, which says the earth was ἀόρατος or invisible, unseen.

9. Bauer, *Greek-English Lexicon*, 94–95; Colossians 1:15–16.

10. Gleick, "Is the Universe Actually Made of Information?," para. 1. "The bit is a fundamental particle, too, but of different stuff altogether: information. It is not just tiny, it is abstract—a flip-flop, a yes-or-no. Now that scientists are finally starting to understand information, they wonder whether it's more fundamental than matter itself. Perhaps the bit is the irreducible kernel of existence; if so, we have entered the information age in more ways than one."

11. Guite, *Faith, Hope and Poetry*, 11.

12. Gleick, "How Information Became a Thing."

and formulae—govern the form and physical behavior of rocks, tides, chipmunks, and everything else we see, alive or inanimate. Our indescribably complex software, networks, recording devices, and broadcast capabilities have enabled the information "cloud" to form—a vast array of binary, digital information representing our photos, songs, business documents, finances, literature, and more that must be housed in material form but in itself remains invisible.[13] A few key values of the physical properties of the universe (the electromagnetic force, the strong force, the weak force, and the gravitational force) preserve it from collapse, locate our planet in the livable zone around our sun, and keep that planet spinning in a way that both distributes heat and gives us days, seasons, and years (such "time" is just another form of metadata).

All this information governs our individual existence and our environment. It is the invisible mind that orders the chaos into a cosmos, that imposes form on matter. No wonder "theoretical physicists are Platonists."[14]

So here we are, flesh-and-blood critters—handfuls of dust plus a few gallons of water—but simultaneously superstructures of inconceivably complex cells, both human and foreign[15]—who are, somehow, awake to our world and the invisible information that pervades and maintains it. What is more, we are each troubled—consciously or not—by questions about our origin, identity, and (especially) destiny. We work hard to come up with rational explanations and answers, but we also depend heavily on imaginative ones.

---

13. Investing material with information requires what physics defines as "work." In the case of digital information, it requires electric power generated by coal, hydropower, and so on; in the case of creation, it requires the power of the Holy Spirit. Every year we have the potential to record more and more information. Is unrecorded information "lost"? It proceeds outward in the form of light, but more than that, all information of ultimate significance must be housed in the mind of God—or it will inevitably perish with the universe.

14. Lightman, "Accidental Universe," para. 5.

15. It is estimated that the foreign cells inextricably linked with our bodies (bacteria, etc.) outnumber human cells by ten to one.

As inescapably, inevitably *embodied* and *storied* humans, both theologians and scientists "prove" their cases through narrative; they live their answers in a narrative way; and they imagine the future in narrative terms.[16] "Whether . . . the writer or writers of Genesis, or of Einstein and Bohr, man has always lived in and by myth."[17] According to Mircea Eliade, "A purely rational man is an abstraction; he is never found in real life."[18] We need both facts and stories; principles and experiences; ideas and images; science and poetry. The invisible and the visible—*logos* and *mythos*.

---

16. In fact, "narrative possibility" and "symbolic reference" may be the unique characteristics of human consciousness (versus animal consciousness). Kruglinski, "What Makes You," paras. 9, 21.

17. Vivas, "Myth," 341.

18. Ibid., 344.

2

What Is a Myth?

AMONG MYTH THEORISTS, NOTHING is as persistent as the recurring statement that *myth* is difficult to define. Michael Fishbane put it this way: "Myth is that most elusive of cultural forms—forever avoiding the constraints of definition and analysis; yet always attesting, through its protean persistence, to an indomitable grip upon the human imagination."[1] The many essays collected in Robert Segal's *Theories of Myth* mostly avoid the overwhelming burden of attempting to define myth outright and comprehensively in a short space. As one writer says, "there are as many definitions of myth as there are mythologists, and as many definitions of reality as philosophers . . . definitions of myth, like myth variants, build up a composite image of something that cannot be said once for all."[2] Another scholar who attempted a "comprehensive definition" of myth listed seventeen different aspects.[3] Let us look briefly at some of the options.

Fiction. It's easy and common to assume that myths are simply stories that no one believes anymore. Knowledge of these stories, especially the Greek or Norse ones, may help with decoding classic literature or writing a blockbuster summer movie, but for the most

---

1. Fishbane, *Biblical Myth*, 1. The adjective "protean" is itself a mythical allusion.
2. O'Flaherty, "Inside and Outside," 279.
3. Doty, "Mythophiles' Dyscrasia."

part it seems that they are a sort of cultural artifact frozen into a past time. Another, increasingly common use of "myth" means "misperceptions that are widely held and need to be exposed"—whether urban legends or diet "myths." This unfortunate usage has robbed the word *myth* of most of its natural connotative power and replaced it with the simplistic meaning "things that aren't true."

Stories about gods. At the next fundamental level, myths are stories about gods.[4] For many moderns and all pure positivists, of course, stories about gods—or God—tend to fall into the "things that aren't true" category. Rudolf Bultmann mentions late in his seminal essay that his demythologizing approach works well as long as you don't have to assume that the referent of the word "God" is also mythical.[5] But this is precisely what many moderns do assume. Those of us who trust and proclaim the Triune God must recognize—yes, and embrace—that our worldview is fundamentally mythical.

More. Some of the many other definitions, descriptions, or theories of *myth* include:

- Protoscientific or protophilosophical explanations or speculations about how our world or specific groups of peoples/cultures came to be (etiology)
- Symbols/signs or allegories for communicating higher knowledge (semiology)
- Expressions arising from the common consciousness of humankind; archetypes (phenomenology)
- A type of speech, a semiological system, a social construct (structuralism)[6]

These are all valid descriptions of myth for various folks at various times, and valuable to bear in mind. They are part of the composite image that is myth.

4. Fishbane, *Biblical Myth*, 27.
5. Bultmann, *Kerygma and Myth*, 33, 43.
6. Barthes, *Mythologies*, 111.

A Modern Difficulty

Because the word "myth" has collected its unfortunate reputation for being simply or even perniciously untrue, it can be difficult for the modern Western reader to access or engage the value of myth. In our post-enlightenment, scientific culture, theologically motivated reports of reality (which includes much of what is contained in Scripture) are considered doubtful by nature. Wherever the scientific sense of history (so-called "objective" fact) is in question, the text's veracity and value is automatically suspect. We have been trained to believe that only a disinterested, objective history is trustworthy and valuable. Furthermore, we assume that the "primitive" ancient mind was incapable of distinguishing superstition and reality—after all, look at the stories these people told. Because the Western mindset is deeply positivistic, we see mythical imagery as having what Rudolf Bultmann called an "apparent claim to objective validity."[7] We assume that mythmakers must either have "really" believed in the three-storied universe—how quaint!—or, in a less condescending mood, we may propose that their imagery was "merely" metaphorical. In either case we dismiss myths' truth claims and value.

Michael Fishbane has some problems with this. His book *Biblical Myth and Rabbinic Mythmaking* is an attempt "to valorize the whole phenomenon of literary and exegetical mythopoesis," which "(as a symbolic form of the imagination) brings a kind of narrative world into being."[8] One of Fishbane's first concerns is to draw his readers outside the most common reductionist approaches to mythology. First he critiques a Greek approach that predates Plato, who "rejected [mythology] for its distortions and illusions" and "morally harmful content"[9]—after all, in the Greek myths you have gods acting in some pretty lousy ways, poor examples for the ideal Republic. Even earlier Greek thought viewed myth as "a fanciful

---

7. Bultmann, *Kerygma and Myth*, 11.
8. Fishbane, *Biblical Myth*, 25.
9. Ibid., 1–2.

way of presenting the truth"[10]—*mythos* as an allegory or bearer of the true word, the *logos*, hidden within. Plato rejected even this notion, preferring to discard all myth, but the approach is intuitive and powerful enough to persist even today in a philosophical worldview profoundly shaped by Hellenistic thought.

Fishbane calls the allegorical approach "a comforting enterprise for those concerned with 'deep structures' and 'rationality,' but a procedure that elides the autonomous and inherent value of mythic imagery and displaces its immediate effects."[11] Here we see that Fishbane is not interested in locating and extracting some elusive truth embedded within myth and discarding the imaginative (or metaphorical) shell, but is instead interested in myth for its own sake. He assumes it has purposes, value, and "effects" of its own.

Fishbane describes two principles that are essential for taking myth seriously. The first is the *principle of parsimony*: similar themes and images that appear in the same "cultural sphere" shall be assumed to have similar effects (even if some appear in, say, Canaanite mythology and others appear in biblical texts where we have a motive for monotheism).[12] The second is the *principle of charity*, which assumes "that every text makes or conveys sense and that one should therefore construe it in the best possible light."[13] This principle guards against the temptation, when finding mythologems (specific mythical themes or topics) in certain genres or contexts, to "in an uncharitable or prejudicial spirit, construe them as mere metaphors."[14] Instead, we should assume "that

10. Ibid., 2.
11. Ibid., 3.
12. Ibid., 17.
13. Ibid., 18.
14. Ibid. Note that there are two very different ways of understanding the term *metaphor*. As Paul Ricoeur describes it, the first and most common is as a literary style, a rhetorical mode of discourse that cloaks an idea in imagery (much like the Hellenistic treatment of myth described above, a "fanciful way of presenting the truth"), an allegory. When this is the case, the imagery can be removed to expose the idea without doing any damage to the meaning of the text; as Ricoeur says, "the literal meaning . . . could have been used in

Systematic Mythology

a mythologem is textually invoked to represent or depict some actual reality."[15] In other words, mythmakers mean what they say. They are attempting to communicate a reality.

But what does the phrase "biblical myth" even mean? How can mythology exist within monotheism? Robert Segal says in his introduction to *Theories of Myth* that Christianity and Judaism are "regularly praised for their nonmythic outlook."[16] Rudolf Bultmann, on the other hand, at least appears to find that the New Testament contains all too much mythology.[17] In the fourth century, Athanasius certainly viewed Christianity as a force that got rid of pagan superstition's chokehold on his world and its residents.[18] Modern fundamentalists view Scripture as containing no

---

the same place." (Ricoeur, *Interpretation Theory*, 49.) This is the understanding that Fishbane is using when he refers to a "mere" metaphor. In contrast, with a "live" metaphor, "a new signification emerges . . . a metaphor is an instantaneous creation, a semantic innovation . . . a new extension of meaning." (Ricoeur, 52.)

15. Fishbane, *Biblical Myth*, 18–19.
16. Segal, *Theories of Myth*, xiii.
17. This is an oversimplification of his views; Bultmann is often misunderstood on this point. His demythologization does not seek to remove myth, but to interpret it in terms of its meaning for existence: "Whatever else may be true, we cannot save the kerygma by selecting some of its features and subtracting others, and thus reduce the amount of mythology in it. . . . the importance of the New Testament mythology lies not in its imagery but in the understanding of existence which it enshrines . . . The New Testament itself invites this kind of criticism. . . . [W]hereas the older liberals used criticism to eliminate the mythology of the New Testament, our task to-day is to use criticism to interpret it. Of course it may still be necessary to eliminate mythology here and there. But the criterion adopted must be taken not from modern thought, but from the understanding of human existence which the New Testament itself enshrines." Bultmann, *Kerygma and Myth*, 9–12.

18. "Did anyone ever fight against the whole system of idol-worship and the whole host of daemons and all magic and all the wisdom of the Greeks, at a time when all of these were strong and flourishing and taking everybody in, as did our Lord, the very Word of God? . . . [T]hose who used to worship idols now tread them under foot, reputed magicians burn their books and the wise prefer to all studies the interpretation of the gospels. They are deserting those whom formerly they worshipped. . . . Their so-called gods are routed by the sign of the cross, and the crucified Savior is proclaimed in all the world as God and Son of God. Moreover, the gods worshipped among the Greeks

What Is a Myth?

mythology at all, only facts; whereas modern atheists view the entire canon as mythological at best (with perhaps some religiously tainted historical value). Who is right?

According to Fishbane, there is a perceived disconnect between the "remnants" of polytheism that exist in the Scriptures and a presumed "pure" monotheism, which is supposed to lack crude, embodied characterizations of deity as well as any references to other contemporary or local mythologies. The distinction between nature gods and supernatural monotheism is so profound, this perspective assumes and (circularly) reasons, that "myth" must be entirely absent from true, pure monotheism.[19]

But Fishbane says this perspective conflates or confuses the literary motive and forms of mythmaking with certain presumed and predefined theological positions. "The exclusive identification of a literary phenomenon (myth) with a specific religious or cultural form (natural polytheism) is both tendentious and tautological."[20] It assumes there is no such thing as mythical monotheistic expression, and thereby impoverishes, misunderstands, and even dismisses much of the Hebrew Bible—especially "its unabashed and pervasive depictions of God in anthropomorphic and anthropopathic terms."[21] Jon Levenson adds: "If, as has often been the case, myth is defined as stories about the gods, then the monotheizing tendencies in the Hebrew Bible exclude myth by definition. Today, this position seems excessively narrow and static and commands little support."[22]

It is worth repeating: as believers in a god—in *the* God—our stance is fundamentally mythical. The last thing we must do is exclude "stories about the gods" from credibility. Levenson continues: "Mythopoesis . . . is a means by which man discerns and conveys truths otherwise inexpressible. If this implication is

---

are now falling into disrepute." Athanasius, *On the Incarnation*, 91–92 (§53). (Circa 318 C.E.)

19. Fishbane, *Biblical Myth*, 5.
20. Ibid., 5–6.
21. Ibid., 6.
22. Levenson, *Sinai and Zion*, 107.

correct, then the familiar interpretation of the religion of Israel as radically demythologized, besides being factually inaccurate, obscures great spiritual treasures."[23]

Fishbane says that imaginative, sensible, concrete accounts of the divine belong to the literary category of myth. He then asks: "Is it even possible to get past the thick immediacy of biblical language and its concrete and sensible accounts of God? . . . [Such] evasions of the direct sense of Scripture . . . must . . . be considered a form of modern apologetics."[24] This form of apologetics belongs to rationalism and post-enlightenment fundamentalism (whether precritical or critical)—to the calculating, rational, positivistic defense of religion on a scientific basis. Such apologetics sees mythical language's "apparent claim to objective validity" and sets to work explaining it away in rational terms.[25] This uncharitable activity kills the myth and finds only historically conditioned metaphors.

Like Fishbane, my project is to "valorize" the idea of monotheistic myth—to explore its manifestations and value, not just for the ancients, but for us today. How can modern Christian believers identify and embrace mythology in Scripture without cognitive dissonance? What role does myth play—now, today—in our relationship with a real, living, and personal God?

In the process, I will remain in conversation with the Nicene and Apostles' creeds as the norm of orthodoxy. *We believe in one God.* . . . My research has also indicated that the literary phenomenon of mythmaking relies on a sacred, authoritative text or texts as the exegetical wellspring for its constructions. Although I will suggest later that there are many such sacred texts, I also wish to be clear that I affirm the Old and New Testaments of

---

23. Ibid., 104–5.

24. Fishbane, *Biblical Myth*, 7.

25. I am not suggesting this activity is unfaithful; most of its practitioners have "faith seeking understanding." It is an instinctive approach for the modern Western student of Scripture. The trouble is that the application of positivistic, scientific criticism—including historical criticism—assumes the atheist perspective by definition. Although such criticism can yield valuable information, it can only explain—or explain away—the text, not interpret its meaning.

the Christian Bible as inspired and authoritative. The Spirit has spoken through the prophets.

As enamored as I am with systematic theology, my current project seeks to enter the growing conversation among post-postmoderns who are no longer satisfied with a positivistic outlook. "In post-modernity everything has the potential to become a symbol but nothing is a symbol of the transcendent.... They do not symbolise a reality in which they participate."[26] We thirst for more.

Systematic mythology is not primarily rational, but imaginative. It is a devotional, rather than a scientific or legal, activity; it wants to experience and not merely describe, to enjoy rather than contemplate,[27] to love rather than rationalize; to live in a sacramental world. Yet it does not abandon the invaluable gains made by historical criticism and orthodox systematic theology.

For a native of the developed Western world, it is impossible, maybe, to move from precritical naïveté anywhere but directly on to critical doubt, like a forced linear move in hopscotch. But it may be possible to take yet another leap, on to something postcritical—to what Paul Ricoeur has called the second naïveté:

> Beyond the desert of criticism, we wish to be called again.... For the second immediacy that we seek and the second naïveté that we await are no longer accessible to us anywhere but in a hermeneutics; we can believe only by interpreting. It is the 'modern' mode of belief in symbols, an expression of the distress of modernity and a remedy for that distress.[28]

Anselm very accurately defined theology as faith seeking understanding. But once some degree of understanding is achieved, faith longs to move on to love, and to tell a story about its Lover. In the end, the mythical includes everything—visible and invisible—that is creatively brought into the story of God. Myth brings a narrative world into being: this is God's world, I am a creature of

---

26. Paul Avis, as quoted in Guite, *Faith, Hope and Poetry*, 9.
27. C.S. Lewis's favorite language for this dilemma.
28. Ricoeur, *Symbolism of Evil*, 352.

God, I have a God. My story is a myth. And living out of that myth has effects in the visible world.

A Working Definition

Back to the question: what is a myth? Michael Fishbane's definition is a solid starting point:

> [W]e shall understand the word "Myth" to refer to (sacred and authoritative) accounts of the deeds and personalities of the gods and heroes during the formative events of primordial times, or during the subsequent historical interventions or actions of these figures which are constitutive for the founding of a given culture and its rituals.[29]

This project will additionally claim that myths are formative in an individual's life and constitutive of his or her actions, attitudes, and personal narrative. They include the events, texts, and heroes that shape an individual's narrative world.

I suggest that mythology is the articulation of a creative, imaginative, and above all *personal* relationship with a divine Subject. Mythmaking creatively exegetes a sacred text to form particular, concrete, contextualized images and accounts of the divine, including or especially human relationship to the divine. The mythical is anything that has been brought into the story of God and God's creature, that is, myself. It includes sacraments, stories, other people, objects, and my body. It informs, and even constitutes, my identity in a profound way.

Notice that I am not referring to any set of specific stories, but to the way stories are generated, interpreted, and come to constitute identity and relationship.

Systematic mythology is *not* a theory of comparative mythology such as Joseph Campbell's work, in which he identifies and conflates similar images or narrative features from varying global

---

29. *Biblical Myth*, 11.

What Is a Myth?

traditions.[30] According to Fishbane, "there is no abstract myth"[31]—a statement that he emphasizes several times as he describes what we might call a principle of particularity:

> There is no abstract myth, but only and always its concrete manifestation in numerous shapes and styles.... It is ... utterly egregious to construct or posit a hypermyth out of the variants of any given myth.... [T]he very notion that these variants are superposable features of a given mythic type ignores the syntax of images in any rendition of a myth and the way it constructs meaning. These elements are the irreplaceable components of its performative particularity.[32]

Instead, I hope to define salient features of the mythmaking motive and describe them in monotheistic terms for application to the modern perspective and practice. Here, "mythology" is not a corpus of material (a noun) but an activity (a verb), used in the same way we use the word "theology." Like systematic theology, this project comes "from faith for faith"; its goal is not primarily evangelistic nor apologetic, although it certainly aims to support faith and the vitality of our proclamation.

Systematic *theo*logy assumes God and abstracts the rules of orthodoxy. Systematic *myth*ology turns the whole of the world into a story about God. It makes my world into a world in which I have a God. It consciously and unconsciously casts everything in this light: the world is a creation, I am a creature, I have a god, I am in relationship with God. My world, and thus my self, is defined by a story about God.

Faith claims that this mythical reality is in fact reality. Yet our picture of this reality is often distorted and sometimes completely off base. Humans have failures of imagination, and we mislocate significance. This is what we call "sin" or idolatry. (More on this later.)

---

30. Campbell, *Hero with a Thousand Faces*.
31. Fishbane, *Biblical Myth*, 16.
32. Ibid., 22.

Myths have to do with the core of who we are; they speak to the ultimate relationship we have with God and to the narrative world we inhabit. Whatever does not speak to these ultimates is not myth, although it has the possibility of being brought into myth. We will describe later that there is no significance outside Christ and no image that does not reflect his image. Whatever is outside Christ or distorts his image is untrue and sinful.

Myths are languaged images or narratives about the gods or God that are significant and imaginative. They are *significant* because they treat our ultimate concern and our relationship to the ground and limits of our existence.[33] They are *imaginative* because they invest visible material with significance via a creative exegetical process.

Let us now look in depth at the two key terms: *significance* and *imagination*.

---

33. The language of "ultimate concern" and the "ground and limits of existence" is per Tillich, *Systematic Theology*, 14. It will be developed more fully below.

3

Significance

MYTH THEORIST ELISEO VIVAS says "the term 'significance' is one of those terms I call 'harlot words,' which is to say, words that work on any street in which they can get away with it, offering themselves . . . without discrimination."[1] It is easy—and extremely common—to call something *significant* without giving any clear indication of what is meant. Let's take a look at several of the faces this harlot word puts on.

First, the dictionary: *significance* means "the quality of conveying or implying; the quality of being important."[2] When something is described as "significant," our immediate questions should include: Conveying *what*? Important to *whom*? (It is telling that the dictionary's first definition says "something that is conveyed as a meaning often obscurely or indirectly").

Things that are important or significant "matter" to us. They "shape" our actions, attitudes, and beliefs. As embodied humans, we take what is significant and let it inform our identities. When significant persons or even things are taken from us, we experience loss and grief and the need to restructure our identities, including our personal narratives.[3] Invisible information—ideas—are put to

---

1. Vivas, "Myth," 346.
2. Merriam-Webster.
3. Kelley, *Grief*, 80–82.

19

work in our lives, and have visible effects in the material world, when they "make sense" or "matter" to us.

This is evident when we look at the "indomitable grip" Fishbane says myths have on the human imagination. First, and most simply, we keep putting classic myths into new, material forms. We are inspired by the stories and we inspire matter with the stories (as by printing them on paper or commissioning human actors and physical sets to recreate them, then displaying them to crowds of cash-wielding moviegoers). The stories matter to us and we make them matter in the world.

A story that is continually mattering in human minds and culture has a form of life. This is what we mean when we refer to a living text (the Bible being the highest example for Christians). David Tracy refers to such texts as "classic," saying that "to converse with any classic text is to find oneself caught up in the questions and answers worthy of a free mind."[4]

Madeleine L'Engle, who was a scientist as well as a top-notch (Christian) children's author, highlighted the interesting meaning of the intransitive verb "matter" in *A Wind in the Door*. One of her characters, Proginoskes, is a (singular) cherubim who is naturally insubstantial. But in order to interact with earthlings, the cherubim must "matter," that is, materialize, take on substance or matter. When the human girl Meg realizes this, she asks, ". . . if you become visible only for us, why do you have to look so terrifying?" His answer: "Because when we matter, this is how we come out. When you got mattered, you didn't choose to look the way you do, did you?" Mattering has another curious side effect. Proginoskes the cherubim now "matters" to Meg the human. She cares about him and his actions. He has become *significant*, as well as visible, to her.

L'Engle's wordplay allows us to see that significance and meaning are related to what is material. Just as a concept only "makes sense" to me when I "grasp" it, just as I say "Oh, I see!" when I understand—what is meaningful or significant is always

---

4. Tracy, *Plurality and Ambiguity*, 20.

something visible or perceptible. This is why myths are both significant and imaginative.

Myths have to do with the core of who we are because they are our way of making meaning, of "making sense" of our ultimate concern, that which matters to us ultimately.

Ultimate Concern

Ernest Becker's articulation of the basic problem of life is so simple that it may seem almost too obvious: we are afraid of death. But to read his book is to be gripped by the paradox that

> ... there really [is] no way to overcome the *real* dilemma of existence, the one of the mortal animal who at the same time is conscious of his mortality. A person spends years coming into his own, developing his talent, his unique gifts, perfecting his discriminations about the world, broadening and sharpening his appetite, learning to bear the disappointments of life, becoming mature, seasoned—finally a unique creature in nature, standing with some dignity and nobility and transcending the animal condition; no longer driven, no longer a complete reflex, not stamped out of any mold. And then the real tragedy, as André Malraux wrote in *The Human Condition*: that it takes sixty years of incredible suffering and effort to make such an individual, and then he is good only for dying. This painful paradox is not lost on the person himself—least of all himself. He feels agonizingly unique, and yet he knows that this doesn't make any difference as far as ultimates are concerned. He has to go the way of the grasshopper, even though it takes longer.[5]

Becker explains that the conscious human creature is aware of her mortality and burdened by a need to make some kind of meaning.[6] But the more brilliant, subtle, and refined our art or our

---

5. Becker, *Denial of Death*, 269.
6. The creators of the film *Flight from Death* discuss Becker's concept of "mortality salience" in terms of culture. Because we crave meaning and stability, we invest our energy into family, work, patriotism, or other goals or causes.

understanding, the more frightening the specter of death. How can all this unique individuality come to nothing? We have no control whatsoever over our own fate: we are radically contingent (as Psalms 39, 90, and the book of Ecclesiastes describe so well). Paul Tillich describes our ultimate concern:

> *Our ultimate concern is that which determines our being or nonbeing.* Nothing can be of ultimate concern for us which does not have the power of threatening and saving our being. . . . [T]he whole of human reality, the structure, the meaning, and the aim of existence. All this is threatened; it can be lost or saved. Man is ultimately concerned about his being and meaning. "To be or not be" in *this* sense is a matter of ultimate, unconditional, total, and infinite concern.[7]

Athanasius too explains that we are "essentially impermanent" and that we do "not just die only, but remain in the state of death and of corruption."[8] We are "held in slavery by the fear of death" (Hebrews 2:15). In short: We are alive, and we have to die, and we know it.

Ernest Becker concludes that the only way of making peace with existence is to "cultivate the passivity of renunciation to the highest powers"[9] . . . to make a gift of oneself to "the life force."[10] He says that "we want nothing less than justification;"[11] that is, we want to know our god on earth and subsume our significance under the heading of that stronger one.

Robert Jenson adds an interesting point about our ultimate significance that goes well beyond the simple ending of an individual's personal story and strivings:

We hope that these causes will outlast us, and we take refuge in the illusion of immortality that they offer. Thus the predefined roles and rules of society offer meaning, validation, and a sense of security.

7. Tillich, *Systematic Theology*, 14. Original emphases.
8. Athanasius, *On the Incarnation*, 28 (§3).
9. Becker, *Denial of Death*, 174.
10. Ibid., 285.
11. Ibid., 173.

Significance

[The] cessation of my consciousness is for me the same as there not being and there never having been and there not going to be anything at all. The actual vanishing of my consciousness is not darkness or unconsciousness; it is not even a void; it is that there is nothing—also not nothingness—and never was anything and never will be anything. . . . The cessation of my consciousness, if it happens, is the retroactive vanishing of being, the sheer occurrence of non-being.[12]

It may seem hopelessly self-centered at first, but give this some thought. For each one of us, our death means the death of the cosmos. The persistence of the universe is acceptable on an objective level, but from a subjective point of view, it is totally meaningless. From the only perspective I can access, the logical result of my eventual death, if it results in oblivion, means that nothing at all will ever exist or has ever existed.

C.S. Lewis describes the logical end of even the objective perspective on the universe, without the creating and saving activity of God: "All stories will come to nothing: all life will turn out in the end to have been a transitory and senseless contortion upon the idiotic face of infinite matter."[13] Given enough time, the universe will either collapse into a new singularity or spread out into a scurf of insubstantiality that is infinitely thin, dead, and cold. Either way, nothing of significance—no information of any kind—will persist. This is why physicist and theologian John Polkinghorne says that "[o]nly a great new act of God can deliver the universe and ourselves from ultimate futility."[14]

There are two primary implications of this materialist view (itself a myth!) of the doomed universe: cosmic and personal. If there is no Creator, then humankind alone (as far as we know) is able to imagine and assign meaning to the universe. There is no objective standard that can say that we are wrong. In its way, this is a kind of Pascal's Wager for the materialist. But it's not much of

---

12. Jenson, *Thinking the Human*, 3.
13. Lewis, *Problem of Pain*, 15.
14. Polkinghorne, *Faith of a Physicist*, 2.

a wager, because the materialist knows that our value assignments must ultimately perish as surely as each of us will. And given Jenson's description of the implications of "my" death, the end of both cosmic and personal meaning is in some ways identical. Thus humanity and the human individual are burdened with the awful responsibility of making meaning for the cosmos. "Quite literally, we are the fallout of the stars . . . we are the only ones in the cosmos who will be able to tell its story and say what it *shall mean*. . . . If nature's great tale is one of absurdity, if it is a blessing or a curse, it depends on us."[15] Humanity also bears the burden of knowing that any such story will finally come to nothing.

Anxiety and Art

According to Rudolf Bultmann, Paul in the New Testament sees that the life of humanity is weighed down by anxiety.[16] "Every man," Bultmann says, "focuses his anxiety upon some particular object. The natural man focuses it upon security, and in proportion to his opportunities and his success in the visible sphere he places his 'confidence' in the 'flesh' (Phil. 3:3f), and the consciousness of security finds its expression in 'glorying.'"[17] This anxiety, which Ernest Becker calls "mortality salience," leads us to deny death and make meaning by placing significance in the visible sphere: seeking (ultimately unobtainable) security by constructing a cosmic, national, or personal narrative and then trusting in it to yield a kind of immortality.[18] Yet this activity—what Paul calls "glorying in the flesh"[19]—is precisely what Becker says we must *not* do if we wish to avoid neurosis and despair.

15. Toolan, "Praying in a Post-Einsteinian Universe," 450, 469.
16. He cites 1 Corinthians 7:32ff.
17. Bultmann, *Kerygma and Myth*, 18.
18. Hence the rise of culture.
19. "'Flesh' embraces not only the material things of life, but all human creation and achievement pursued for the sake of some tangible reward, such as for example the fulfilling of the law (Galatians 3:3). It includes every passive quality, and every advantage a man can have, in the sphere of visible, tangible

Significance

According to Becker, the artist is in special danger of understanding her "agonizing uniqueness." The more creative she is, the greater her art and her awareness of its greatness, the greater the burden of anxiety.[20] Eberhard Jüngel explains it this way:

> Man discovers the contradictions and the meaninglessness around him deeply rooted within himself, and thus for him the world which is so overly weighted with his own subjectivity moves perilously close to the edge of futility into which it threatens to fall—and because the world is his responsibility, he will be responsible for that fall.[21]

Yet, Becker says, we "must live with agonizing doubts if [we are to remain] in touch at all with the larger reality."[22] The denial of death provides a temporary haven for the anxious mind, but it does not change the reality that each of us will die. Trusting in our own art—narrative constructions—mythopoetry—becomes idolatry precisely because we look to it for life and what Becker calls justification. "We want redemption—nothing less. . . . We want to be justified, to know that our creation has not been in vain."[23] Because she knows her art is ultimately futile (what Ecclesiastes calls "vanity of vanities," הֲבֵל הֲבָלִים) and cannot justify or give ultimate life, the artist must continue to bolster that art in whatever ways she can—that is, she serves her god.

What is the solution? Again, according to Becker, "the only way out of the human conflict is full renunciation, to give one's life as a gift to the highest powers."[24]

Part of the good news Christianity offers to the postmodern positivist is that we have a Creator. This good news is not based on an objective, literalist understanding of Genesis 1 "imagery with

---

reality (Phil. 3:4ff)." Bultmann, *Kerygma and Myth*, 18.

20. Becker, *Denial of Death*, 172.
21. Jüngel, *God as the Mystery of the World*, 53.
22. Becker, *Denial of Death*, 196–97.
23. Ibid., 167.
24. Ibid., 173.

its apparent claim to objective validity."[25] We shall not understand such imagery as a scientific report,[26] but as a narrative that is *significant* and *imaginative*.[27] Instead, we turn to Isaiah 46:4, where we find God's claim: "I have made, and I will bear; I will carry and will save." Unlike our personal narratives and constructions, unlike our idols, the true God is our creator: the only one with the power to justify, and the only god who does not need our service. "If I were hungry, I would not tell you!"[28] Instead, characteristic of the only Creator God is that the Lord does the creating, saving, and justifying. Recall that "the Lord" stands for the revealed personal name of God, which roughly means: "I am what I am; I will be what I will be; I cause what I cause."

The only way out of the human conflict, Becker says, the only solution to our overwhelming and dreadfully realistic mortality salience, is to "admit creatureliness."[29] That means understanding my story, my life, my existence, as a radically contingent creature who depends upon a powerful Creator, the only one who is able to rescue me from ultimate insignificance. I cannot be the hero of my own story;[30] I must not pretend to be my own creator. Justification

---

25. Bultmann, *Kerygma and Myth*, 11.

26. Augustine said in the late fourth century: "In matters that are obscure and far beyond our vision, even in such as we may find treated in Holy Scripture, different interpretations are sometimes possible without prejudice to the faith we have received. In such a case, we should not rush in headlong and so firmly take our stand on one side that, if further progress in the search for truth justly undermines this position, we too fall with it." Augustine, *Literal Meaning of Genesis*, 41 (18.37).

27. Origen said in the third century: "I do not think anyone will doubt that these are figurative expressions which indicate certain mysteries through a semblance of history and not through actual events." Origen, *On First Principles*, 288.

28. Psalm 50:12a. The verse continues, "For the world and all that is in it is mine." See also Acts 17:24–25: "The God who made the world and everything in it, he who is Lord of heaven and earth, does not live in shrines made by human hands, nor is he served by human hands, as though he needed anything, since he himself gives to all mortals life and breath and all things."

29. Becker, *Denial of Death*, 173, 197.

30. More on heroes below.

Significance

requires living in a narrative world whose Subject is God; it means the systematic mythologizing of the cosmos, not as a story about the creature, but about the Creator.[31]

Christian apologists are normally quick to refute the atheist objection that religion is "a fairy story for people who are afraid of the dark," as physicist Stephen Hawking put it, but in fact we should admit or even embrace the truth in this claim. We are telling a story in which the dark does not win; a story that proclaims the endurance of all that is meaningful, beautiful, beloved, significant, and living; that says hope is a legitimate choice versus ultimate futility. We are telling a story about a God who is able to save. That many of us find this story preferable to the dark does not, by itself, make it untrue.[32]

Each of us needs to make meaning; each of us finds some way to address our ultimate concern. This is not only a private desire, but a human inevitability. (When asked "how we should live," even Stephen Hawking followed up his fairy-story comment with an admonition to "seek the greatest value of our action."[33] How shall we define such value?) Mortality, not sin, is the theological concern of the modern positivist. Yet they are two sides of the same coin.

In fact, there is apparently no logical problem with ultimate meaninglessness, but we still have a lot of trouble with it. As Paul Tillich explains: "The individual man passionately asks that he be allowed the possibility of believing in a personal fulfillment in spite of the negativity of his historical existence."[34] There are two possibilities: either I am the author of my own story, which will lead

---

31. Athanasius agreed with this appraisal of our core problem—our ultimate concern. He saw that the creation is tending, through idolatry, back to non-being, and that the only one with the power, authority, and responsibility to rescue it is God, our creator. *On the Incarnation*, 31–32 (§6); see note 36 on page 78.

32. The rejection of Christ may be too often caused by a misperception of what Christianity is about. Strict seven-day creationism is a modern construct, not a requirement for faith in the Creator God or the redemptive work of Christ. See notes 26 and 27, previous page.

33. Hough, "Stephen Hawking: 'Heaven Is a Fairy Story,'" paras. 9, 10.

34. Tillich, *Systematic Theology*, 266.

Systematic Mythology

to overwhelming anxiety and ultimate insignificance, or God is the Author of all our stories, and has the power to assign ultimate significance and give abundant life.[35] I cannot bear the weight of telling the universe's story; God can.

I have not addressed the vital question of *truth* in addition to this pragmatic question of what we need or what we actually do. I believe that it is true that God is our creator. But for the purposes of this project, I wish to highlight that God alone has the power to justify, to vivify, to signify—in a word—to save.

Heroes versus Mortals

Michael Fishbane's definition of myth included "accounts of the deeds and personalities of the gods *and heroes*." Let us take this opportunity to discuss the meaning of "hero" from the perspective of Ernest Becker.

Becker discusses heroism in connection with a human phenomenon called transference. A hero is a person whom we imaginatively burden with responsibility for providing meaning in our lives and security from death. Transference is when we project these feelings of ultimacy onto another person. Becker says that it is a tremendous relief to the tension of mortality salience to identify one's god on earth and to imagine that satisfying him or her satisfies our ultimate concern. "If you don't have a God in heaven, an invisible dimension that justifies the visible one, then you take what is nearest at hand and work out your problems on that."[36] Nearest of all, of course, is the self. Next best (early in life) is a parent; later, a romantic partner or a therapist.

"Transference is a universal passion," Becker says. "It represents a natural attempt to be healed and to be whole, through heroic self-expansion in the 'other.'"[37] Yet, unless this transference is focused on Christ, it is both idolatry and a danger—humans do

---

35. God "gives life to the dead and calls into existence the things that do not exist" (Romans 4:17).
36. Becker, *Denial of Death*, 162.
37. Ibid., 157.

not have the power to justify; they invariably disappoint as either heroes or gods.

Fascinatingly, Becker uses the language of "redemption" and "justification" to describe our attempts to find meaning:

> After all, what do we want when we elevate [another person] to the position of God? We want redemption—nothing less. We want to be rid of our faults, of our feeling of nothingness. We want to be justified, to know that our creation has not been in vain.[38]

By "justified," Becker does not mean the forensic (judicial or legal) state of forgiveness that cultural Christianity often assumes. Instead he means something much closer (though not identical) to the Lutheran theological description of justification as the right relationship of creatures with our Creator, looking to God alone for life. Only the Creator can justify a creature's existence. Looking to my parent, partner, child, or any other human mortal as the hero of my life's story becomes idolatry, not only because I have assigned that person the role of god of my life, but also because that person *cannot* bear the imaginative burden. Every human disappoints as hero, except one: the only son of God, Jesus of Nazareth, the Christ. As Psalm 146:3–6 puts it:

> Do not put your trust in princes, in mortals, in whom there is no help.
>
> When their breath departs, they return to the earth; on that very day their plans perish.
>
> Happy are those whose . . . hope is in the Lord their God, who made heaven and earth, the sea, and all that is in them; who keeps faith for ever.

Each of us must consciously locate all virtue (in the sense of the philosophers' *arete*, excellence) in Jesus Christ, the only Son of Man in whom there is "help" or salvation, and place all our trust in God, the creator of heaven and earth. We are free and indeed required to love our neighbor, but no human can fill the role of

---

38. Ibid., 167.

ultimate source of virtue, meaning, and wholeness. God alone gives life. Whatever virtue I love in my neighbor, or my hero, has Christ as its source and ultimate location.

Live Wire

Another aspect of significance is that it is subjective and contextual (that is, particular). Philosopher William James suggests that when we hear a new idea, we find it to be either alive or dead, much like an electrical wire you might find in your wall.[39] If it is dead, there is nothing about your idea that can move me to trust, embrace, or even take interest in it. If it is alive, this signals that I partially believe it already. Something within me recognizes your idea as a possibility and maybe even a desirable one.

Mythology has a similar quality. Certain stories or images resonate with us; regardless of their historical accuracy, there is something about the story that is important, that is alive, that matters. Indeed, there is an evolutionary quality at work here: those narratives that no longer matter are, by definition, abandoned. Karen Armstrong believes that religion is highly pragmatic in this area.[40] In other words, if sacred stories and the cultic activities (rites) that express them—what we today might call organized religion—were not significant to us, we would have abandoned them by now (and they may yet change).

Paul Tillich explains in *Dynamics of Faith* that true symbols cannot be produced or invented artificially. "Symbols do not grow because people are longing for them, and they do not die because of scientific or practical criticism. They die because they can no longer produce response in the group where they originally found

---

39. James, *Will to Believe*, 2.

40. Armstrong, *History of God*, xxi. Armstrong asks: "Is modern atheism a similar denial of a 'God' which is no longer adequate to the problems of our time? Despite its otherworldliness, religion is highly pragmatic. . . . [I]t is far more important for a particular idea of God to work than for it to be logically or scientifically sound. As soon as it ceases to be effective it will be changed—sometimes for something radically different."

expression."[41] What is significant or alive to any person or group has deep roots in our animal, cultural, and individual contexts.

Our worldview is composed of narratives and images that are "alive," that matter to us, that create desire and compel faith. The result is a system of meaning, a *Weltanschauung* or worldview. Bultmann says, "Of course such a view is not absolutely unalterable, and the individual may even contribute to its change. But he can do so only when he is faced by a new set of facts so compelling as to make his previous view of the world untenable. He has then no alternative but to modify his view of the world or produce a new one."[42]

Informed Substance

Eliseo Vivas contributes another useful idea to the myth theory we are developing: that of "informed substance." First of all, he says that myths are "stories that organize the primary data of experience."[43] This is true of both religious and "cognitive" pictures of the world; "no philosophical picture is totally positivistic," he says, because we feel the need "always to exist in a total and organized world, in a cosmos." Even our most scientific *Weltanschauungen* are constructed out of "many old bricks and beams,"[44] and guided by the same impulse as the most ancient stories: that of adding meaning or significance to the matter that exists around us. Vivas explains further:

> Symbols are the product of a synthesis of our intuitions or impressions, received by the mind, selected and added to in order to achieve informed substance that is present to it as experience. . . . Before the newborn's mind this matter consists of uninformed intuitions deriving from his sensory responses to the external

---

41. Tillich, *Dynamics of Faith*, 43.

42. Bultmann, *Kerygma and Myth*, 31. He is speaking here about the obsolescence of the premodern mythical worldview.

43. Vivas, "Myth," 95.

44. Ibid., 100.

world. But these responses make no sense to him. As his mind develops, the "matter for" experience is trans-substanced as it is informed. . . . It is this informed substance that the mind grasps and calls its world. . . . There is no world, out there or inside, for us, unless it has been constituted by the mind.[45]

Interestingly, the physicist Brian Greene kicks off *The Fabric of the Cosmos* with a similar meditation. He begins by discussing his encounter as a youth with the myth of Sisyphus as retold by Camus; discovers that its central question is that of suicide, in other words, whether life is worth living;[46] and realizes that this really is the central question for individual human life. "To this aspiring physicist," he says, "it seemed that an informed appraisal of life absolutely required a full understanding of life's arena—the universe."[47] And today, as a physicist who has firmly arrived? "Assessing existence while failing to embrace the insights of modern physics would be like wrestling in the dark with an unknown opponent. By deepening our understanding of the true nature of physical reality, we profoundly reconfigure our sense of ourselves and our experience of the universe . . . our picture of reality."[48]

Is the allusion to Jacob's wrestling with God (the foundational event for "Israel," which means "struggles with God,"[49]) a coincidence? That seems unlikely.[50] Regardless of that, though, we note the same language of myth and "picture of reality," the same quest

---

45. Ibid., 95.

46. This is also a central concern of William James in *The Will to Believe*—not to mention the title of the once wildly popular television series *Life Is Worth Living* with Bishop Fulton Sheen.

47. Greene, *Fabric of the Cosmos*, 4.

48. Ibid., 5.

49. Genesis 32:28.

50. As Marilynne Robinson has said: "The Bible is the model for and subject of more art and thought than those of us who live within its influence, consciously or unconsciously, will ever know. Literatures are self-referential by nature, and even when references to Scripture in contemporary fiction and poetry are no more than ornamental or rhetorical—indeed, even when they are unintentional—they are still a natural consequence of the persistence of a powerful literary tradition." Robinson, "Book of Books," paras. 1, 2.

for significance, in even the most highly trained, positivistic (what Vivas calls "philosophical") mind. David Tracy explains: "The dream of positivism was to discover a reality without quotation marks: a realm of pure data and facts.... Positivism tried to deny what neither Newton nor Einstein, neither Planck nor Heisenberg ever denied: the fact that even science itself is interpretation."[51]

It seems that the "matter for experience" is not significant or meaningful in itself. It requires a mind—a person—to construct, organize, and assign meaning. As Tracy puts it, "Reality is what we name our best interpretation.... [It] is constituted, not created or simply found, through the interpretations that have earned the right to be called relatively adequate or true."[52] This kind of interpretation and value assignment is certainly done by humans; Vivas points out that it is also done by God: "And God saw the light, that it was good."[53] Naturally, the value assignment of the Creator is of far greater significance, having ontological effect, compared to that of humans. I suggest, though, that part of God's redemptive work in creation is saying "yes" to some of our value assignments[54]; that God has deliberately populated the created universe with meaning-makers whose efforts will, through Christ, ultimately enrich God's creation.

Vivas says that "the mind that responds to [certain objects] in the religious mode of experience discerns in them their sacred quality or nature."[55] We invest our surroundings with significance, whether by telling stories about troll-shaped mountains in Iceland, building high and magnificent cathedrals, or by developing

---

51. Tracy, *Plurality and Ambiguity*, 47–48.

52. Ibid., 48.

53. Vivas, "Myth," 102. "It was not until some four thousand years later, by the pre-Darwinian calendar, that old Hobbes corrected the writer of Genesis. The light was not in itself good. God merely thought it was good, because the light was an object of his appetite or desire. I submit that the biblical myth is considerably more adequate to the actuality of our experience of values than the lucubrations of old Hobbes."

54. 2 Corinthians 1:20: "For in him every one of God's promises is a 'Yes.' For this reason it is through him that we say the 'Amen,' to the glory of God."

55. Vivas, "Myth," 101.

sentimental attachments to our personal belongings. Our imaginations are constantly at work developing, signifying, and organizing our personal cosmos.[56] Done in light of our god, this discerning and investing becomes systematic mythologizing.

The church fathers believed that whatever is not assumed, that is, taken up, in Christ's incarnation is not redeemed, but that whatever Christ does assume is saved.[57] (The word "deem" means to judge or determine value. Thus, whatever is assumed and re-deemed by Christ enters God's eternal life.) The combination of God's value assignment and God's gracious assumption through Christ of our value assignments results, I suggest, in the "subjective truth" of the universe. It is composed, maintained, and multiplied by minds, by persons, and ultimately by the Triune God.[58] In this sense, the universe is still becoming a cosmos. When all things are summed up in Christ, the living Word of God, when death and the powers that objectify have disappeared back into nothing, all of reality will truly be a Subjective, "informed substance." This is the promise of Habakkuk 2:14: "the earth will be filled with the knowledge of the glory of the LORD, as the waters cover the sea."

The knowledge of the glory of the LORD has to do with God's presence and deeds, with God bearing the "heavy" burden of our existence (in Hebrew, "glory" also means "weight" or "heaviness"). When we promote ourselves or others as idols, we deny that God is carrying us and ascribe that glory elsewhere; we fall short of the glory. This is true too when we worry about tomorrow and allow

---

56. As we will see below, though, they are also too often at work misplacing significance and objectifying the neighbor.

57. "For that which He has not assumed He has not healed; but that which is united to His Godhead is also saved. If only half Adam fell, then that which Christ assumes and saves may be half also; but if the whole of his nature fell, it must be united to the whole nature of Him that was begotten, and so be saved as a whole." Gregory of Nazianzus, Epistle 51, in Schaff, *Nicene and Post-Nicene Fathers* (Second Series), 440.

58. 1 Corinthians 8:6: "For us there is one God, the Father, from whom are all things and for whom we exist, and one Lord, Jesus Christ, through whom are all things and through whom we exist."

our devices and scheming[59] to overwhelm us with fear—enslaving us to death—instead of trusting in God's providence, wisdom, plans, and power. Again, God says, "I have made, and I will bear; I will carry and will save."[60] God has done exactly that in the person and work of Jesus Christ. Nothing is left but for us to love the truth.[61] This is what it is to have a God.[62]

---

59. More on this below as "imagination."
60. Isaiah 46:4b.
61. 2 Thessalonians 2:10b.
62. "[T]hrough Christ . . . we now truly realize that we have a God . . . we call upon him, give thanks to him, and love him." Melanchthon, Apology of the Augsburg Confession, Article IV: Justification, §141, in Kolb et al., *Book of Concord*, 142.

4

Imagination

FROM "SIGNIFICANCE" WE NOW move on to the other key aspect of mythology: imagination. Myth's imaginative quality is surely one of its most apparent features. From the Norse creation myth in which the world is formed out of the skull of a slain god who emerged out of an abyss of ice and fire, to the well-known Greek myths about gods and heroes, to the extravagant pantheon of Hinduism's living faith—the imagery of myth appeals to our physical senses and pleases our creative instinct. Yet this is the same characteristic that causes it to be dismissed. As one biblical scholar put it, "The ancient myths are serious but imaginative attempts to explain life in this world."[1] With that little conjunction, "but," we see the whole frowning disposition of the Western reductionist, positivistic mind when it beholds works of the imagination. Life in this world, it says, cannot be explained imaginatively, but only scientifically.[2]

Yet, the imagination is the interface through which we interact with the world and each other. Whether we are daydreaming, composing an important memo to our employer, exercising brand loyalty, picturing the farthest expanses of the cosmos, or demanding that our partner do the dishes, our imaginations are at work: assigning significance, multiplying meaning, applying narrative

---

1. Collins, *Hebrew Bible*, 30.

2. Of course, good science requires plenty of imagination in order to make new connections and discoveries.

qualities to events, and influencing our behavior, attitudes, and actions. We imagine others in terms of their value to us, what we suppose their motives and feelings toward ourselves to be, and where we assign their significance in our personal narrative cosmos—whether we imagine them as heroes or as slaves. As Tillich says, "We transform reality according to the way we see it, and we see reality according to the way we transform it."[3]

Poetry

Myth theorists tend to mention narratives and images in a way that is basically interchangeable. This has to do with myth's close connection to poetry. Both myth and poetry are languaged images; both can be narrative. Both the brief, recurring mythical themes that Fishbane calls "mythologems" and longer, self-contained narratives rely heavily on imagery, on language that is sensible (perceptible to the senses). As mentioned earlier, Michael Fishbane says such language has "thick immediacy"; myths are "concrete and sensible" accounts of gods or God. Kirstin Jeffrey Johnson, a scholar of George MacDonald's "mythopoetic" art, calls myths "storied images."[4] The famous poet and student of myth Robert Graves defined myth "in its strict sense of 'verbal iconograph.'"[5] I find the word "iconograph" especially appropriate in light of Jesus' question in Matthew 22:20 (my translation): "Whose image and inscription is this?" In Greek, the question (Τίνος ἡ εἰκὼν αὕτη καὶ ἡ ἐπιγραφή;) includes the elements of iconograph: εἰκὼν (image) and γραφία (writing). We will see later that Jesus asks this question not only about coins, but also about each one of us.

Myths are verbal iconographs (narrative or languaged images). Like poetry, they are composed of sentences—*sent*ence meaning that which bears sense, which imparts meaning. They call

---

3. Tillich, *Systematic Theology*, 76.

4. Jeffrey Johnson, "Rooted in All Its Story," 154.

5. Graves, *White Goddess*, 7. The sentence continues: ". . . without the derogatory sense of 'absurd fiction' that it has acquired."

up images; some are almost aggressively physical.[6] This is why—despite being made of invisible words and language—they fall on the visible side of the visible/invisible philosophical divide. Indeed, we can even associate the term "visible word" from Augustine's definition of sacrament: "The word is added to the element, and there results the Sacrament, as if itself also a kind of visible word."[7]

A narrative or languaged image describes an experience of some reality; it re-presents it to our senses. It is a form of metadata in that it is not the experience itself, but information about the experience; yet to hear a narrative or see an image is itself an experience. Thus a narrative is not a formula of logic, but it is still a "word" in the sense of *mythos* versus *logos*. A narrative or image is, in its own particular way, an abstraction; it is a representation of something, created either in words or in material. It is used by its poet (its maker) to add significance or meaning—interpretation—to the bare fact of events or existence.

Thus, narratives and languaged images—poetry—are both "pictures" that signify or point to something else. Keeping Michael Fishbane's principle of charity in mind, we will assume that "something else" has reality.

Eliseo Vivas said, "Myth is to be used for stories that organize the primary data of experience . . . they are pictures of the world within which and by which men live."[8] Bultmann emphasizes, "The real purpose of myth is not to present an objective picture of the world as it is, but to express man's understanding of himself in the world in which he lives." He continues:

> Mythology is the use of imagery to express the other worldly in terms of this world and the divine in terms of human life, the other side in terms of this side. . . . Myth speaks of the power or the powers which man supposes

---

6. I am thinking here of the physical language in the Enuma Elish or the Atrahasis, but it also applies to Michael Fishbane's accounts of biblical myth: language that is concretized, particular, and immediately sensible.

7. "Homilies on the Gospel of John," Schaff, *Nicene and Post-Nicene Fathers* (First Series), 344.

8. Vivas, "Myth," 95.

IMAGINATION

he experiences as the ground and limit of his world and of his own activity and suffering. He describes these powers in terms derived from the visible world, with its tangible objects and forces, and from human life, with its feelings, motives, and potentialities."[9]

To add a thought from Tillich:

> The symbols of faith do not appear in isolation. They are united in 'stories of the gods,' which is the meaning of the Greek word 'mythos'—myth. . . . Myths are stories of faith combined in stories about divine-human encounters . . . [using] material from our ordinary experience . . . [they put] the stories of the gods into the framework of time and space although it belongs to the nature of the ultimate to be beyond time and space.[10]

Language of ultimacy, language that describes the horizons of experience where the world we see touches the singularities we cannot see, is always mythopoetic. This is especially true of texts that describe origins and endings; see Genesis, Revelation, and all the wild prophetic imagery in between.[11] Yet it is also true, if in more subdued fashion, of the prosaic workings of everyday life and the personal metanarrative of the now.

Giving Form to Thought

The Christian novelist, poet, and preacher George MacDonald was particularly interested in the function and cultivation of the imagination. He defined it in this way:

> The word itself means an imaging or a making of likenesses. The imagination is that faculty which gives form to thought—not necessarily uttered form, but form capable of being uttered in shape or in sound, or in any mode upon which the senses can lay hold. It

---

9. Bultmann, *Kerygma and Myth*, 10.
10. Tillich, *Dynamics of Faith*, 48–49.
11. See also the *Urzeit* and *Endzeit* stories of other myth systems.

is, therefore, that faculty in man which is likest to the prime operation of the power of God, and has, therefore, been called the creative faculty, and its exercise creation. Poet means maker.[12]

Of course there is a profound division between the original, prime Creator and human "sub-creators" (to use J.R.R. Tolkien's word[13]). We work only with what is given: our world, its inhabitants, and their stories. Kirstin Jeffrey Johnson explains:

> MacDonald—like those he influences—argues that *creatio ex nihilo* is in the domain of the Divine Maker only. . . . Through engagement with inspiration [creative humans] respond to what they have found in God's creation. Stories evolve from the response of the writer/teller to external forces (humans, animals, nature); a story is an expression of relationship that seeks to relate.[14]

This relational element is what makes the imagination a close partner with significance. It is an attempt at communication. It signifies something to someone—something worth communicating.

> How shall the one show the other that which is invisible? . . . [H]e seizes [a] symbol, as the garment or body of his invisible thought, presents it to his friend, and his friend understands him. Every word so employed with a new meaning is henceforth . . . born of the imagination and not of the understanding, and is henceforth submitted to new laws of growth and modification.[15]

According to Jeffrey Johnson, MacDonald believed "that an understanding of the intrinsically relational God cannot be grasped outside of a relational hermeneutic; that a list of dry propositions would never be able to convey what the fullness of

---

12. MacDonald, *Imagination*, 2.

13. See Tolkien's seminal essay "On Fairy-Stories," available in *Tree and Leaf*. (This essay is also the source of the wonderful word "eucatastrophe.")

14. Jeffrey Johnson, "Rooted in All Its Story," 19.

15. MacDonald, *Imagination*, 8.

poesis could."¹⁶ "To understand," he posits, "is not more wonderful than to love."¹⁷ As Bultmann put it: "The unseen, intangible reality actually confronts us as love, opening up our future and signifying not death but life."¹⁸ Love—charity, agape—is the proper work of the imagination.¹⁹

The Invisible God

What about imagining God? A persistent and interesting theme of the Christian Bible is God's invisibility juxtaposed with a continual desire to view God or God's likeness.

Scripture insists that God is invisible, which is comforting since this is certainly the case, much as we might wish it were otherwise. Although the Scriptural examples are not numerous, they are emphatic. Interestingly, explicit statements about God's invisibility are confined mostly to the New Testament; the Old Testament is basically satisfied with implying invisibility.

> **John 1:18** No one has ever seen God.
>
> **1 John 4:12** No one has ever seen God.
>
> **Romans 1:20** Ever since the creation of the world [God's] eternal power and divine nature, invisible though they are, have been understood and seen through the things [God] has made.
>
> **1 Timothy 1:17** To the King of the ages, immortal, invisible, the only God, be honour and glory for ever and ever.
>
> **1 Timothy 6:16** [RSV] Who alone has immortality and dwells in unapproachable light, whom no man has ever seen or can see.

16. Jeffrey Johnson, "Rooted in All Its Story," 6.
17. Ibid., 48. Quoted from *Lilith*.
18. Bultmann, *Kerygma and Myth*, 19.
19. Through participation in Christ and by acting in Christ's image, Luther says that "a Christian becomes a skillful artisan and a wonderful creator, who can make joy out of sadness, comfort out of terror, righteousness out of sin, and life out of death." Mannermaa, *Christ Present in Faith*, 44.

> **Hebrews 11:27** By faith he left Egypt, unafraid of the king's anger; for he persevered as though he saw [the one] who is invisible.
>
> **Colossians 1:15** He is the image of the invisible God.

In the last verse, from Colossians, we have a hint of what is to come—the abundant satisfaction of all our desire to behold God.[20]

In contrast to these New Testament statements, we find several instances of folks in the Old Testament who are said to have "seen God," including Adam, Eve, Hagar, Jacob, Abraham, and of course Moses, to name a few. Often, what they saw is described as "the angel of the LORD," preserving the assertion that God is profoundly invisible.

Despite this, there is abundant witness in the Old Testament to something called God's image, God's likeness, God's face; even God's beauty. The Psalms are replete with expressions of the fervent desire to behold God—a desire that would be unnecessary if God were simply visible (or *simply* invisible). According to Jon Levenson, "There is a very real sense in which the deity is visually available in the Temple, this in spite of all the insistence that one cannot see God and that his reality cannot be captured in an image."[21]

> **Psalm 27:4, 8** One thing I asked of the LORD, that will I seek after: to live in the house of the LORD all the days of my life, to behold the beauty of the LORD, and to inquire in his temple. . . . "Come," my heart says, "seek his face!" Your face, LORD, do I seek. Do not hide your face from me.
>
> **Psalm 42:2** My soul thirsts for God, for the living God. When shall I come and behold the face of God?

In its continuing desire to behold God, the Hebrew Bible provides many, not "graven," but mythical images. Michael Fishbane associates the "concrete and sensible accounts of God" in the

---

20. Christ and the promise of resurrection fulfills the confident statement of Psalm 17:15: "As for me, I shall behold your face in righteousness; when I awake I shall be satisfied, beholding your likeness."

21. Levenson, *Sinai and Zion*, 95.

IMAGINATION

Hebrew Scriptures with myth.[22] The ancient Hebrews eschewed graven images, but they reveled and abounded in mythopoetic descriptions. These could also be called metaphors—but an inspired, scriptural metaphor is more than a literary style. It communicates a reality; it is an instrument God uses in self-revelation to us creatures. The God of the Hebrew Scriptures is invisible, but also close, real, palpable to the senses; even "bluntly physical."[23] You can feel this God holding your hand:

> **Psalm 73:23** I am continually with you; you hold my right hand.
>
> **Isaiah 41:13** For I, the LORD your God, hold your right hand; it is I who say to you, "Do not fear, I will help you."
>
> **Psalm 22:9** Yet it was you who took me from the womb; you kept me safe on my mother's breasts. [See also Psalm 71:6.]
>
> **Psalm 16:8-9** I keep the LORD always before me; because he is at my right hand, I shall not be moved. Therefore my heart is glad, and my soul rejoices; my body also rests secure.
>
> **Psalm 17:8** Guard me as the apple of the eye; hide me in the shadow of your wings.
>
> **Psalm 63:8** My soul clings to you; your right hand upholds me.

We are overlooking a reality—reading uncharitably—if we assume such witnesses are "merely" metaphorical. According to Fishbane, "[i]t would hardly make sense to reduce the divine hand to a mere metaphor or the sea monsters to allegorical figures—as if these images are simply the product of an inability to speak abstractly. Within the literary and religious framework of [Psalm 74, in this case], both images partake of a vivid mythic

---

22. Fishbane, *Biblical Myth*, 7.
23. Jenson, *Ezekiel*, 283. He is describing God's words to Israel in Ezekiel 37:12: "I am going to open your graves, and bring you up from your graves, O my people."

realism whose facticity the speaker hardly doubts. This is, in fact, a core element of the psalmist's hope."[24]

The charitable reader will assume that the psalmist is describing a reality, an experience of relationship with the invisible God. Fishbane points out that "the evasions of the direct sense of Scripture . . . must . . . be considered a species of modern apologetics."[25] As explained earlier, such apologetics belongs to rationalism and post-enlightenment fundamentalism, not to the imaginative, personal relationship with God that we are seeking to describe—and inhabit.[26]

Fishbane's idea of Scriptural myth may be summarized in a statement he quotes from *Genesis Rabba* 27.1: "Great is the power of the prophets; for they liken a form (*tzurah*) to its Creator."[27] Fishbane describes this as warm praise in favor of the ancient prophets' "power to envision the figure of God upon His throne in the very form (human) which He himself created in his own (divine) image." For examples, see Isaiah's vision of God's throne; Ezekiel's vision of God's chariot; Psalm 18; and any number of other instances in which the invisible God is imagined in immediate, palpable terms.

Making Images

The first, most justly famous mention of God's image comes in Genesis when God creates humans.

> **Genesis 1:26a** Then God said, "Let us make humankind in our image, according to our likeness."

---

24. Fishbane, *Biblical Myth*, 41.

25. Ibid., 7.

26. This type of apologetics—the evasion of the direct sense of Scripture out of misplaced deference to the demands of positivism—must be distinguished from the ἀπολογία of the faith as described in 1 Peter 3:15: "Always be ready to make your defense to anyone who demands from you an accounting for the hope that is in you."

27. Fishbane, *Biblical Myth*, 8.

IMAGINATION

This is imagination as the "imaging or making of likenesses." In creation, God's imagination has not only produced a cosmos, but also taken dust and made "living souls" (לְנֶפֶשׁ חַיָּה)—male and female earthlings, human beings made in the image of God.[28]

But then came the disaster: humans in turn began to make likenesses—and worship them as if they were gods:[29]

> **Psalm 106:20** They exchanged the glory of God for the image of an ox that eats grass.

This type of imagination—the making of images that are then given the highest significance, worshipped, and set up as gods—directly opposes God's intention. Although humans have the glory of being made in God's image and are given dominion over fish, birds, cattle, and everything that creeps on the earth, instead of worshipping God, humans give up that glory and freedom and bow down to images of creatures made of wood or metal.

Of course, this is echoed in the first chapter of Paul's letter to the Romans:

> **Romans 1:22–23** Claiming to be wise, they became fools; and they exchanged the glory of the immortal God for images resembling a mortal human being or birds or four-footed animals or reptiles.

Twice now we have the idea that humans exchange the glory of God for idols. I initially described that glory as being the glory of being created in God's image. There is also the glory of freely worshipping the living Creator God as opposed to an inert statue,

---

28. This is sometimes taken as "proof" that we humans have created God in *our* image, but faith insists that the biblical account is correct. Moreover, Christian faith asserts that we are created by God in the image of Christ, a human like us who is actually "the express image of God." As Luther said, in the Incarnation, it is true that "God is a human being, and a human being is God"(!). Formula of Concord, in Kolb et al., *Book of Concord*, 510.

29. And ascribed to them the credit for salvation: "[Aaron] took the gold from them, formed it in a mold, and cast an image of a calf; and they said, 'These are your gods, O Israel, who brought you up out of the land of Egypt!'" (Exodus 32:4).

not to mention the sense in which "glory" indicates the very presence or saving activity[30] of God. But there is more.

At least twice we have a clear statement that those who worship dead, insensible images "are like them" (as opposed to being "like" the image or glory of God):

> **Psalm 115:4-9** Their idols are silver and gold, the work of human hands.
>
> They have mouths, but do not speak; eyes, but do not see.
>
> They have ears, but do not hear; noses, but do not smell.
>
> They have hands, but do not feel; feet, but do not walk; they make no sound in their throats.
>
> Those who make them are like them; so are all who trust in them.

In Psalm 135 we find a similar statement, but with a slightly different emphasis as those who worship idols "become" like them (which is closer to the idea of "exchange"):

> **Psalm 135:15-18** The idols of the nations are silver and gold, the work of human hands.
>
> They have mouths, but they do not speak; they have eyes, but they do not see;
>
> they have ears, but they do not hear, and there is no breath in their mouths.
>
> Those who make them and all who trust them shall become like them.

The point is clear: *we become what we imagine,* much as we are what we eat. And what are idols like? They have mouths, but do not speak, eyes, but do not see, and so on. There is no breath in their mouths. In other words, they are dead.

> **Psalm 49:7-15** [RSV] Truly no man can ransom himself, or give to God the price of his life, for the ransom of his life is costly, and can never suffice, that he should

---

30. As described earlier; see Isaiah 46.

continue to live on for ever, and never see the Pit. Yea, he shall see that even the wise die, the fool and the stupid alike must perish and leave their wealth to others. Their graves *[or imaginations]*[31] are their homes for ever, their dwelling places to all generations. . . . Man cannot abide in his pomp, he is like the beasts that perish. . . . Like sheep they are appointed for Sheol; Death shall be their shepherd; straight to the grave they descend, and their form shall waste away; Sheol shall be their home. But God will ransom my soul from the power of Sheol, for he will receive me.

Our ultimate concern is what concerns us ultimately: "that which determines our being or not being."[32] Death is the very definition of nonbeing, as the consciousness (apparently) ceases, the form wastes away, and the body returns to its dust. But here is the good news: God is the one who "gives life to the dead and calls into existence the things that do not exist."[33] How? The weak and ungodly are saved when they stop beholding and reflecting death. As Athanasius put it: "By nature, of course, man is mortal, since he was made from nothing; but he bears also the Likeness of Him Who is, and if he preserves that likeness through constant contemplation, then his nature is deprived of its power and he remains incorrupt."[34] God reveals Christ to us, and through the power of the Spirit, invites and calls us to behold him as Lord. This is the true image of the living God, the one who planted the ear, who formed the eye, and whose Spirit is the very breath of life.

Colossians 1:15 He is the image of the invisible God, the firstborn of all creation.

---

31. The RSV notes that "imagination" is an alternate translation for "graves." The word is: קֶרֶב n.[m.] "inward part, midst—1. a. *inward part* of human body, physical sense, בְּ *within* one's body; *into* his body; as seat of life. . . . 2. of inward part of man; a. as seat of thought and emotion; seat of לֵב; of רוּחַ. b. as faculty of thought and emotion, subj. (no prep.)." Brown et al., *Hebrew and English Lexicon*, 899.

32. Tillich, *Systematic Theology*, 14.

33. Romans 4:17.

34. Athanasius, *On the Incarnation*, 30 (§4).

Colossians 3:10 [A]nd have clothed yourselves with the new self, which is being renewed in knowledge according to the image of its creator.

1 Corinthians 15:49 Just as we have borne the image of the man of dust, we will also bear the image of the man of heaven.

2 Corinthians 3:18 All of us, with unveiled faces, seeing the glory of the Lord as though reflected in a mirror, are being transformed into the same image from one degree of glory to another; for this comes from the Lord, the Spirit.

Romans 8:29 Those whom he foreknew he also predestined to be conformed to the image of his Son.

2 Corinthians 4:4 In their case the god of this world has blinded the minds of the unbelievers, to keep them from seeing the light of the gospel of the glory of Christ, who is the image of God.

1 John 3:2 When he is revealed, we will be like him, for we will see him as he is.

Idolatry is deadly not only because it is an error and a sin to worship the creature rather than the Creator, but because we become conformed to the image that is constantly before us, to which we dedicate our lives, the "picture we use for living." By conforming ourselves to that which is dead, we die.[35] As Jesus said, if your inner light is darkness, how great is that darkness![36]

When we imagine ourselves as the originators of the cosmos, as gods or God, we exchange the glory of God's likeness for the likeness of animals that eat grass. This is a failure of imagination: idolatry, sin. This is how we fall short of the glory of God.[37] The cure is when the Holy Spirit causes us to behold Christ—the crucified

---

35. Jonah 2:8 says the same thing another way: "Those who worship vain idols forsake their own mercy." [Combination of NRSV and KJV. The Hebrew is: [מְשַׁמְּרִים הַבְלֵי־שָׁוְא חַסְדָּם יַעֲזֹבוּ]

36. Matthew 6:23.

37. Romans 3:23.

and risen one, the image of the invisible God—as Lord: "And the Word became flesh and lived among us, and we have seen his glory, the glory as of a father's only son, full of grace and truth.... From his fullness we have all received, grace upon grace."[38]

"For it is the God who said, 'Let light shine out of darkness,' who has shone in our hearts to give the light of the knowledge of the glory of God in the face of Jesus Christ."[39] This is our hero and our God.

Planning or Devising

Although the dictionary labels it "archaic," one of the definitions of imagination is to "plan or scheme."[40] In the beginning, God spoke light and everything else into being. At first, the earth was unformed, or in Greek, ἀόρατος, "invisible" (LXX). Yet the power of the Holy Spirit is in manifesting the invisible.

Several Scriptures attest that God made the cosmos "by understanding."[41] The Bible makes it clear that God has purposes and plans for creation. Using the Hebrew word מַחֲשָׁבָה (thought, device, or plan)[42] as a guide to compare the "imagination" of humankind with the plans and purposes of God is revealing.[43]

> **Genesis 6:5** [RSV] The LORD saw that the wickedness of man was great in the earth, and that every imagination [מַחְשְׁבֹת] of the thoughts of his heart was only evil continually.

---

38. John 1:14, 16.
39. 2 Corinthians 4:6.
40. Merriam-Webster.
41. Proverbs 3:19; Jeremiah 10:12 and 51:15; Psalm 136:5; Job 26:12; Isaiah 40:28.
42. Usually διαλογισμός in Greek/LXX. Surveying this term is also revealing.
43. The word's close relationship to artistic "imagination" is evident in contexts such as Exodus 31:4: "to devise artistic designs [מַחְשָׁבֹת], to work in gold, silver, and bronze" [RSV].

Systematic Mythology

> Isaiah 59:7 Their feet run to evil, and they rush to shed innocent blood; their thoughts are thoughts [מַחְשְׁבֹתֵיהֶם מַחְשְׁבוֹת] of iniquity; desolation and destruction are in their highways.

> Psalm 94:11 The LORD knows our thoughts [מַחְשָׁבוֹת], that they are but an empty breath [הָבֶל].

We see that humanity's plans and devices are "evil," that they bring death, and that they are ultimately "empty."[44] "Evil" is that which objectifies being: "[Evil transforms] living being into objects to be manipulated, and since a living being dies when it becomes an object, evil is a force against life."[45] Instead of imagining others as being made in the image of God and as those for whom Christ died—subjects—we look at them as objects: means to some end, servants, or worse. Such objectification, when it is mature,[46] makes it possible to "rush to shed innocent blood." As with the making and worshipping of false images, this type of imagination is empty (vanity, הָבֶל) and leads only to death and meaninglessness.

Compare this to the imagination of God, who gives life to the dead and calls forth being out of nonbeing; to God's Spirit, which is also a "breath" (or more properly, a "wind," רוּחַ rather than הָבֶל). God's breath[47] is full of potential and has the power to manifest that potential. Paul Tillich described *life* as "the process in which potential being becomes actual being" and *spirit* as "the unity of power and meaning."[48]

> Proverbs 19:21 The human mind may devise many plans [מַחֲשָׁבוֹת], but it is the purpose of the LORD that will be established.

---

44. Compare Ephesians 3:19: "and to know the love of Christ that surpasses knowledge, so that you may be filled with all the fullness of God."

45. Gustafson, *Evil*, 31. As quoted in Splichal Larson, *A Witness*, 237.

46. See James 1:14–15: "But one is tempted by one's own desire, being lured and enticed by it; then, when that desire has conceived, it gives birth to sin, and that sin, when it is fully grown, gives birth to death."

47. God also gives "the breath of life," נִשְׁמַת חַיִּים (Genesis 2:7).

48. Tillich, *Systematic Theology*, 249.

IMAGINATION

> **Psalm 33:10-11** The Lord brings the counsel of the nations to nothing; he frustrates the plans [מַחְשְׁבוֹת] of the peoples. The counsel of the Lord stands for ever, the thoughts [מַחְשְׁבוֹת] of his heart to all generations.
>
> **1 Chronicles 28:9b** [T]he Lord searches every mind, and understands every plan and thought [מַחֲשָׁבוֹת]. If you seek him, he will be found by you; but if you forsake him, he will abandon you for ever.
>
> **Jeremiah 29:11** For surely I know the plans [הַמַּחֲשָׁבֹת] I have for you, says the Lord, plans [מַחְשְׁבוֹת] for your welfare and not for harm, to give you a future with hope.
>
> **2 Samuel 14:14** We must all die; we are like water spilled on the ground, which cannot be gathered up. But God will not take away a life; he will devise plans [מַחֲשָׁבוֹת] so as not to keep an outcast banished for ever from his presence.

God's imagination does its proper work of love; it creates living beings out of dust; and even when humanity sets up its own gods, objectifies its neighbors, and embraces its own death and destruction, God imagines ways to salvage our ultimate concern, to save—that is, *redeem*—our being. "When we were yet without strength, in due time Christ died for the ungodly."[49] In the words of Psalm 103:2-4:

> Bless the Lord, O my soul,
> and do not forget all his benefits—
> who forgives all your iniquity,
> who heals all your diseases,
> who redeems your life from the Pit,
> who crowns you with steadfast love and mercy.

---

49. Romans 5:6 [KJV].

5

Mythopoesis

We have seen that mythology uses the narrative form to imaginatively invest meaning into reality. A myth is a significant and imaginative narrative that a society or individual uses to articulate (and reinforce) its origins, role, and destiny. According to Eliseo Vivas:

> Today it is generally agreed that myth making is a permanent activity of all men, an activity that men apparently cannot live without.... To say man lives in myth is to say that the picture of the world within which he lives is at least partly mythical; to say that he lives by myth is to say that he uses that picture for living.[1]

Mythology is thus fundamental to a person's identity; it is the "picture we use for living," and it brings our "narrative world" into being. And—lest we forget—myths are stories about God.

The Stories We Live By

Of course, the word "mythology" invokes a whole host of images and stories that already exist in our world and culture. According to Dan McAdams in *The Stories We Live By: Personal Myths and the Making of the Self*, each individual creates a myth of her own using

---

1. Vivas, "Myth," 89.

the texts available to her. His claim is that "identity is a life story";[2] he says that "through our personal myths, we help to create the world we live in, at the same time that it is creating us."[3]

Each human person is born into a world that is already rich with context. Each one of us spends our "formative" years becoming familiar with our native language, culture, physical environment, and family story via the innumerable and diverse texts that comprise our early education and entertainment. According to McAdams, "Throughout our preschool years, we are unwittingly collecting and stockpiling images."[4] (To use William James' language, we collect those images that are "alive" to us.) McAdams continues, "By the time we reach young adulthood, we have accumulated a veritable treasure trove of personalized symbols and fantasized objects. As adults, we draw creatively upon the imagery in fashioning our personal myths."[5]

Thus, these images come to have profound significance to our identities; they are combined over a lifetime in a way that provides "*unity* and *purpose*."[6] Unity refers to narrative coherence. As psychotherapist and Wartburg Theological Seminary pastoral care professor Dan Olson has said, "We are deeply uncomfortable if we don't have a narrative, because without it life feels fragmented and episodic." But what is the purpose? McAdams says we desire "to expand, preserve, and enhance the self as a powerful and autonomous agent in the world, and to relate, merge, and surrender the self to other selves within a loving and intimate community."[7] He is being a little optimistic here; we have already seen, per Becker, that we cannot bear the anxiety of being our own hero, and we have also seen that the natural imagination views the neighbor as a slave or an object. Still, McAdams' insight is important: we seek

---

2. McAdams, *Stories We Live By*, 5.
3. Ibid., 37.
4. Ibid., 55.
5. Ibid.
6. Ibid., 24. Emphasis mine.
7. Ibid., 68.

both security (that is, power) and love, and our efforts to create those things are narrative in nature.[8]

Melissa Kelley has written about grief and the human need to make meaning after great loss. She too approaches this from the perspective of story, saying that "Each of us . . . creates our own life stories. . . . [T]hey express how we understand ourselves."[9] Like McAdams, she means this quite literally: each of us is telling ourselves the story of our lives, complete with plot, theme, characters, time and timing, continuity, and sense/coherence. A major loss can disrupt each of these elements of a person's story, leaving her in "narrative freefall,"[10] uncertain of her identity.

Granted that we each construct life "stories" out of available imagery and other resources, how does this narrative become a myth? McAdams says that "[m]yths incorporate archetypal symbols that remain viable today if our imaginations are active enough to make us conscious of, and curious about, our origins and destiny. . . . To say that a personal myth is 'sacred' is to suggest . . . [that it] deals with those ultimate questions that preoccupy theologians and philosophers."[11] A personal myth is the imaginative articulation of relationship with our ultimate concern (God).

We saw earlier (per Tillich and James) that symbols are not constructed artificially but are found already existing in our narrative environment. "By the time we begin to compose our personal myth, we are predisposed [by what we were attracted to as children] to create our identities along certain thematic lines."[12] McAdams is suggesting that we are each drawn to certain available symbols, including (or especially) those present in our religious traditions. "Judeo-Christian religious traditions contain a wealth

---

8. He also offers the intriguing idea that "the good life story is one of the most important gifts we can ever offer each other," and that "the most mature personal myths are those that enhance the mythmaking of others." Ibid., 7, 113.

9. Kelley, *Grief*, 80–81.

10. Ibid., 82.

11. McAdams, *Stories We Live By*, 34.

12. Ibid., 75.

of compelling images that are repeatedly imported, with strong emotional associations, into personal myths."[13]

"Mythopoesis . . . is a means by which man discerns and conveys truths otherwise inexpressible."[14] If McAdams and Kelley are right, there is a close relationship between the literary activity of mythmaking and the personal activity of identity-making. In each case, we collect significant images and snippets of our storied environments and use them to construct a narrative that expresses the core of our identity—our role in our narrative world. The literary mythmaking motive and the personal or religious mythmaking motive are thus the same: each seeks to relate to our ultimate concern (the one who determines our being or nonbeing), which leads us inevitably to the only hero with the power to assign ontological significance. Thanks to our personal myth, "We are tethered in an ultimate sense to a loving, cherishing God who holds us and protects us from the threat of meaninglessness."[15]

According to McAdams, "One of the virtues [of studying personal myth] is making conscious a personal predilection for viewing the world, which may previously have seemed part of the nature of the world and not of the self."[16] He says that "In order to understand our own myths, we must explore the unique way in which each of us employs imagery to make sense of who we are."[17]

Our identities and worldview—our personal myths—are thickly embedded with significant stories and imaginative, constructed meaning.[18] This being the case, it is essential to examine how these stories come to be and ensure that we are building them out of the best possible materials—neither misplacing significance, nor relying on failures of imagination.[19] Then, we must ask

13. Ibid., 64.

14. Levenson, *Sinai and Zion*, 104–5.

15. Kelley, *Grief*, 90. "Tethered" also connotes the original meaning of "religion"—to tie, to bind together.

16. McAdams, *Stories We Live By*, 53.

17. Ibid., 55.

18. Each personal mythology is also unique (or particular).

19. Note that these risks are exactly why Plato wanted to exclude poets

whether and how our stories, as an essential part of our selves, are redeemed in Christ.

The Exegetical Imagination

Mythmaking, or mythopoesis, is a process of the religious imagination that exegetes sacred texts in order to develop relational significance. It develops images or narratives that promote relationship with God.

Let us look at two examples of monotheistic mythmaking that are both literary and religious: rabbinic and romantic mythopoesis.

Rabbinic. Recall that one of the goals of Michael Fishbane's book *Biblical Myth and Rabbinic Mythmaking* is "to valorize the whole phenomenon of literary and exegetical mythopoesis," which "(as a symbolic form of the imagination) brings a kind of narrative world into being."[20] Exegesis is central to this activity: "Myth is kept alive by its uses and reuses, as it moves from context to context and serves different cultural or individual needs. . . . [Mythmaking is] a learned and literary act that . . . is a sign of ongoing cultural creativity."[21] In the Midrash and the medieval book of *Zohar*, Fishbane explains, "an ancient literary thesaurus was remoulded by learned acts of textual exegesis."[22]

Used in this way, the word "thesaurus" is identical with the "treasure trove" that McAdams describes—indeed, it's the same word in Greek (θησαυρός).[23] Elsewhere Fishbane calls myth "a

---

from his ideal Republic.

20. Fishbane, *Biblical Myth*, 25.
21. Ibid., 20.
22. Ibid., 21.
23. See also Matthew 13:52: "Therefore every scribe who has been trained for the kingdom of heaven is like the master of a household who brings out of his treasure (θησαυροῦ) what is new and what is old." And Matthew 12:35 (or Luke 6:45): "The good person brings good things out of a good treasure, and the evil person brings evil things out of an evil treasure."

fund of dramatic images about the gods."[24] Particularly in the Midrash, which is the "commentary" of rabbinic Judaism, myths and mythopoesis "are based on a closed, canonical Scripture, whose every word and phrase can serve as the basis of new mythic inventions . . . all [sacred topics] are given new mythic resonance through exegetical fabulations of God's role in sacred history."[25] This process, Fishbane says, culminates in the *Zohar*, where "the vast *traditum* of Judaism is taken over as a resource for a powerful and protean mythopoesis built out of the language of Scripture . . . the new fabulations draw upon all the natural images, personalities, and reports found in the scriptural source and transform their meaning and essence."[26] A rich thesaurus, indeed.

Fishbane explains that rabbinic mythopoesis uses several techniques. One is the concretization of the language of Scripture, which is "mythopoesis that turned the invisible into the visible."[27] Another is textual correlation, which serves to deepen and multiply the meaning of "terse and exalted" language in Scripture.[28] For example, Fishbane describes how R. Judah creatively correlates texts:

> Quite dramatically, the formal account of Genesis 1 is given mythic depth through correlation with other passages in Scripture. . . . [T]he exegete at once reveals a mythic core to Genesis 1 while at the same time re-valorizing mythic images found elsewhere in the biblical text. For the sage, mythic accounts are in truth a more visible and tangible version of the secrets of beginnings. . . . At least according to R. Judah, myth is another language of God's primordial acts, even one that goes deeper into the unknown and portrays the living drama of creation. . . . *Myth is itself exegesis, a mode of inspired imagination.*[29]

24. Fishbane, *Biblical Myth*, 3.
25. Ibid., 26.
26. Ibid.
27. Ibid., 104.
28. Ibid., 103.
29. Ibid. Emphasis mine.

Along with imagination, we have seen that "significance," or the development of relationship with our ultimate concern (God), is one of the two major aspects of mythmaking. In a section titled "Myths of Participation and Pathos," Fishbane describes the rabbinic exegetical mythmaking process by which God is revealed to identify with God's people. For example, he spends several pages on the theme of God's "withdrawn arm."[30]

The process begins with a difficult text, Lamentations 2:3b: "[H]e has withdrawn his right hand from them in the face of the enemy." This is a lament that God has withdrawn God's powerful protection, allowing the invasion and destruction of Israel. Yet through creative exegesis, Fishbane explains, other texts are correlated with this lament: texts that promise God's everlasting sympathy with the people of Israel, along with a concretizing midrash that declares, "the Holy One (thus) said, . . . as long as my children are in servitude, My right hand shall be in bondage; (and) when I redeem My children, I redeem my right hand."[31]

This "midrashic myth" allows the original lament to be creatively re-read as marking "the onset of divine compassion *after* the siege." The myth demonstrates that God's right arm was withdrawn, not to abandon Israel to its enemies, but because God's right hand would be in bondage until Israel would be redeemed and freed. "[N]ow we have a myth of divine participation and sympathy wrested (exegetically) from a lament of judgment."[32] No text can withstand the rabbis' determined exegetical efforts to reveal God's steadfast love.

Romantic. George MacDonald may be called the primogenitor of a special flavor of mythopoesis that is familiar to students of such famous Christian storytellers as C.S. Lewis, J.R.R. Tolkien, and Madeleine L'Engle. Lewis called MacDonald his "master" and said his *Phantastes* "baptized my imagination." L'Engle said MacDonald both shaped and saved "her understanding of God and her ability

---

30. Ibid., 147–49.
31. Ibid., 148.
32. Ibid., 149.

to be an artist."³³ Tolkien was less directly influenced by MacDonald but was very much an advocate of the "sub-creative" activity of mythmaking. Kirstin Jeffrey Johnson has carefully analyzed the "relational and revelational nature of George MacDonald's mythopoeic art,"³⁴ and her work reveals the importance of the exegetical imagination in romantic mythmaking.³⁵

According to Jeffrey Johnson, MacDonald believed that both writing and identity arise out of an individual's particular relationships and community. He believed that to understand what an author is communicating (and assuming, in the spirit of Fishbane's "principle of charity," that writing *is* an attempt at communication), is to empathize, and to seek to empathize, with that author.³⁶ Jeffrey Johnson reports that "MacDonald's own declared aim as a literary critic is to better facilitate the relationship 'betwixt my readers and the writers from whom I have quoted.'"³⁷ In MacDonald's mythopoetic efforts, he aimed to facilitate the relationship between his readers and the writer from whom he is quoting—the very Author of creation.

The imagination, says MacDonald, "has created none of the material . . . But it takes forms already existing, and gathers them about a thought so much higher than they, that it can group and subordinate and harmonize them into a whole which shall represent, unveil that thought."³⁸ This unveiling is imagining the

33. Jeffrey Johnson, "Rooted in All Its Story," xv.

34. This is the thesis subtitle for Jeffrey Johnson, "Rooted in All Its Story."

35. I am calling all of these authors "romantic" (lower case "r"); they wrote romances in the classic sense of "a prose narrative treating imaginary characters involved in events remote in time or place and usually heroic, adventurous, or mysterious" (Merriam-Webster). None were true Romantics, yet all of them share the Romantic esteem for the imagination and value the "numinous" (that is, the awful yet profoundly desirable presence of the divine Other—what the Romantics labeled "the sublime," Rudolf Otto called "the holy," and the Bible calls "the fear of the LORD"). Thus, an element of the sublime is common to mythopoetic fantasy fiction.

36. Ibid., xx.

37. Ibid.

38. MacDonald, *Imagination*, 20.

invisible: taking invisible thought and embodying it in new and unique ways that are perceptible to the senses, that "make sense," and that develop relationship. The grouping, subordinating, and harmonizing is exegesis of the "text." The relationship developed—with other humans, with other stories and texts, and ultimately with God, the source—is what I have called "significance."

C.S. Lewis has been accused of writing pastiche—of quoting too freely from too many traditions—but his work too is exegesis of a larger text.[39] Again, the symbols and language that speak to us (that are significant) are never merely artificial, but organic. We must refer to, invoke, or embody them—we cannot produce them. Thus mythopoesis is not creation out of nothing, but exegesis of an authoritative, sacred text;[40] human creativity is not (as we tend to suppose today) mere originality, but is original (or *particular*) exegesis or embodiment of significant, storied images.

Even when MacDonald believed a storyline was "received" (as with *Lilith*), in his compositions he "brought a lifetime of relational engagements and careful exegesis. . . . [H]e invites revelation to function on multiple levels of time, space, and experience. He is convinced that the particularities of the text, even if never decipherable, will not hinder the heavily storied Story. . . . The stories help to exegete the stories."[41] To bring Fishbane back into this for a mo-

---

39. Especially in view of Lewis's continuing power to communicate the divine—something mere pastiche could not accomplish. Only a profound knowledge of the text can construct myths of profound power. See Michael Ward's exquisite *Planet Narnia* for an exploration of Lewis's profound, and profoundly coherent, approach to mythopoesis.

40. No doubt the first authoritative texts (if we can speak in terms other than the Word) are phenomenological or natural ("we all have the same kinds of dragons in our psyche, just as we all have the same kind of hearts and lungs in our body" [O'Flaherty, "Inside and Outside," 303]), graciously inspired by the Spirit to unite the visible and invisible. Eventually you have something like the liturgy which is enacted mythology, exegeted from Scripture and experience, saturated with millennia of meaning. As described by Jeffrey Johnson: "To stand in a tradition of Story is both to receive and to be part of 'passing on' that which is infused with the truths of myths that have gone before" (Jeffrey Johnson, "Rooted in All Its Story," 18).

41. Jeffrey Johnson, "Rooted in All Its Story," 243.

Mythopoesis

ment: "The 'work' of myth . . . is as much a matter of deliberation as of spontaneous intuition; as much a product of fixed genres and phraseology as of innovative combinations or mixed forms."[42]

We have seen that both rabbinic and romantic mythmakers focus on a canon or sacred text as the exegetical wellspring for their constructions. Rabbinic mythopoets focused on a closed canon of Scriptural texts,[43] while romantics added literary, traditional, and scientific sources, inviting us to explore the open canon of our cosmos. The rabbinic mythopoet focuses on the deeds, character, and compassion of the LORD; the Christian romantic focuses on the one ὅς ἐστιν εἰκὼν τοῦ θεοῦ τοῦ ἀοράτου ("who is the image of the invisible God").[44]

In their very different ways, both rabbinic and romantic mythopoets develop relationship with God; they seek to communicate a reality to the alert, storied, and charitable reader. Evident in both is the purpose of multiplying meaning. Thus we see that mythopoesis, whether literary or personally "religious," is profoundly theological. It seeks to relate to the divine in terms of those images that are available and significant to its audience; to transform and deepen that relationship; to multiply its meaning and to enjoy it in new and profound ways.[45]

---

42. Fishbane, *Biblical Myth*, 82.

43. "The myths and mythopoesis found in the Midrash are based on a closed, canonical Scripture, whose every word and phrase can serve as the basis of new mythic inventions. . . . [T]he older biblical mythologems are expanded and correlated with other passages that are read mythically; and the central topics . . . are all given new mythic resonance through exegetical fabulations of God's role in sacred history." Ibid., 26. We should note that biblical myth also includes mythopoesis that is identifiably exegetical, taking material both from the created environment as well as the pagan cultural environment. See especially Genesis 1–2 (bearing traces of the Babylonian primordial myths Enuma Elish and Atrahasis) and Psalm 104 (resonant of Akhenaten's Hymn to the Sun Disk). See also Collins, *Hebrew Bible*, 30–45.

44. Colossians 1:15.

45. It would be interesting to review additional examples of faithful imagination, such as the mystical imagination; the Jesuit spiritual practice of imagination; and the medieval religious imagination. An example of the latter

The Christian may claim that the exegetical imagination is both faithful and valuable when its aim, concern, and desire is to behold and commune with Christ, who is the image of the invisible God. John 1:18 (RSV) says that "No one has ever seen God; the only Son, who is in the bosom of the Father, he has made him known." The word translated "made known" is ἐξηγήσατο (from ἐξηγέομαι), which means "tell, relate, explain, report; make known, reveal."[46] It is the verbal form of ἐξήγησις (exegesis), "narration that provides a detailed description."[47] Thus imaginative, narrative exegesis—faithful mythopoesis—is an activity of the children of God. It is one more way we can follow our Lord: the Word become visible, the *logos* become *mythos*.

Sacred Texts

If the primary method of mythmaking is exegesis of a sacred text, what exactly is a sacred text? A text becomes sacred if it is one that we successfully exegete in order to form our identity and to respond to our ultimate concern. In other words, texts we find to be "alive," that supply the images we need to make sense of our ultimate concern, become sacred to us.

Naturally, this is especially true of the Bible. In a statement that comports with the premise of McAdams' *The Stories We Live By*, Michael Fishbane says that:

> [W]e are, in part, a living texture of ideas derived from our reading—centering points of multiple texts which constitute our interior and exterior worlds. . . . The Bible may become sacred to us insofar as its images and

---

is Charbonneau-Lassay, *The Bestiary of Christ*, which examines the symbolic significance of a range of creatures from the humble to the fantastic, from the sea urchin to the pelican to the unicorn and the ouroboros. The medieval mind was adept at assigning significance to everything visible, from creature to cosmos, and bringing it into the story of Christ. "[Medieval m]an looked up at a patterned, populous, intricate, finite cosmos; a builded thing, not a wilderness; 'heaven' or 'spheres,' not 'space.'" Lewis, *Studies*, 7.

46. UBS Concise Dictionary, page 64, in *UBS Greek New Testament*.
47. Bauer, *Greek-English Lexicon*, 349.

MYTHOPOESIS

language shape our discourse, stimulate our moral and spiritual growth, and simply bind us to past generations which also took this text seriously. Indeed, the Bible may become sacred in this way because—together with other texts—it helps establish our personhood.[48]

According to David Tracy, "To be human is to be a skilled interpreter."[49] Indeed, I would add that we each interpret an incredible range of "texts" every day, and not only written ones. From changes in the weather, to small variations in the shapes of our cars, to tiny differences among human faces and their expressions, to the evocative scents of summer . . . the list goes on and on. Human perception—the metaphorical "eye"—is able to pick up a stunning range of subtlety and nuance. We combine it all into our actions, choices, attitudes—our persons. Thus, a sacred text is one that we interpret to "establish our personhood."

Another characteristic of a "sacred text" is that it is inspired—a controversial term. George MacDonald proposes that because "there is always more in a work of art—which is the highest human result of the embodying imagination—than the producer himself perceived while he produced it, seems to us a strong reason for attributing to it a larger origin than the man alone—for saying at the last, that the inspiration of the Almighty shaped its ends."[50] Scripture, which is "inspired by God"[51] (literally, God-breathed, θεόπνευστος), is the example *par excellence* of such inspiration.[52] As Origen explains:

> The truth of the faith holds that there is one and the same God of the Law and the Gospels, Creator "of the visible and the invisible" (2 Cor 4.18). For the visible holds the

---

48. Fishbane, *Garments of Torah*, 132.

49. Tracy, *Plurality and Ambiguity*, 9.

50. MacDonald, *Imagination*, 25.

51. 2 Timothy 3:16: "All Scripture is inspired by God and is useful for teaching, for reproof, for correction, and for training in righteousness."

52. Merriam-Webster defines inspiration as "a divine influence or action on a person believed to qualify him or her to receive and communicate sacred revelation."

highest relationship with the invisible, as the Apostle says, "The invisible is perceived from the creation of the world through the things that are made" (Rom 1.20). Therefore, just as "the visible and the invisible," earth and heaven, soul and flesh, body and spirit have mutually this kinship and this world is a result of their union, so also we must believe that Holy Scripture results from the visible and the invisible.[53]

To go back to the rabbis and Michael Fishbane: "This reading [of *Pesikta de-Rav Kahana* 4.4] would provide a notion of divine inspiration for the bold acts of human imagination performed by the prophets; that is, their power to imagine God in human terms is itself a God-given power, and no mere human act or capacity."[54] In Christian terms, we would say that the Holy Spirit moved the prophets and poets to speak, and informed their speech with the Word—with the Son. The Spirit works through the reader, too: a student of the Scriptures will always encounter more meaning than the original human author could have foreseen or intended. Yet the new meaning too belongs to the text:

> Scripture (not just the Christian Bible) is a relatively stable category; as fundamentally written text, it has the quality, using the language of Paul Ricoeur, of "semantic autonomy." The text of Scripture is inscribed, and therefore, "the author's intention and the meaning of the text cease to coincide.... The text's career escapes the finite horizon lived by its author. What the text means now matters more than what the author meant when he wrote it." ... Scripture and its interpretations are rooted in time and place, culture and language, but not limited by the finite reality of the author.... Where there are readers, the text will be read and interpreted. In this way, the interpretations of a text *belong* to the meaning of the text itself.[55]

---

53. Origen, *Homilies on Leviticus* 5.1, as quoted in Yarchin, *Biblical Interpretation*, 42. Thanks to Sam Giere for the quote.

54. Fishbane, *Biblical Myth*, 236.

55. Giere, "This Is My World!," 24. He quotes Ricoeur, *Interpretation Theory*, 29–30.

MYTHOPOESIS

Through the Spirit's power and inspiration, both the Old and New Testaments have faithfully revealed the invisible God to countless students of the Bible over the millennia, manifesting to them in new and particular ways God's character, deeds, love, faithfulness, sovereignty, and immanence. The student of the Torah says: "Oh, how I love your law! It is my meditation all day long."[56] The Christian agrees, but also takes seriously Christ's warning: "You search the scriptures because you think that in them you have eternal life; and it is they that testify on my behalf. Yet you refuse to come to me to have life."[57] The Bible is sacred, inspired, and authoritative, but it is not itself the source of life.

Another sacred text is the created world. This is the inspired Book of Nature, the cosmos that God made by understanding[58] through the power of the Holy Spirit and that we all inhabit.[59] "Natural theology" has its drawbacks,[60] but we know that God's invisible nature is perceptible in creation.[61] Thus, we may learn about the incredible creativity and imagination of God by studying the amazing things God has made, and I suggest that we may do that by studying the best science. From black holes to protozoa, calcium in our bones and calcium in the stars, chlorophyll, mitochondria, ambergris, and the hibernating bumblebee queen—"If we had a keen vision and feeling of all ordinary human life, it would be like hearing the grass grow and the squirrel's heart beat, and we should

---

56. Psalm 119:97.

57. John 5:39–40.

58. Proverbs 3:19; Jeremiah 10:12 and 51:15; Psalm 136:5; Job 26:12; Isaiah 40:28.

59. Isaiah 45:18: "For thus says the LORD, who created the heavens (he is God!), who formed the earth and made it (he established it; he did not create it a chaos, he formed it to be inhabited!): 'I am the LORD, and there is no other.'"

60. Including inherent ambiguities, such as disasters and disease, and a reliance (by definition) on historically conditioned understandings of how the physical world really works—understandings that change, sometimes radically, as we learn more.

61. Romans 1:20.

die of that roar which lies on the other side of silence."[62] Science delves into, delights in, and displays it all.

Finally, we may also attribute inspiration—the living work of the Holy Spirit—wherever we find storied images that cause us to behold Christ and acknowledge him as Lord and God. This happens perhaps most frequently and clearly—or at least, most intentionally—in the proclaimed word, the gospel, in which a preacher unites the particular context and concerns of a congregation and its members with a text or texts from the Bible, and does so in light of the crucified Christ. It happens each time any believer shares the good news that Jesus Christ is Lord in the narrative terms that make sense to him or her. But the Holy Spirit is also able to work through classic literature, including the sacred stories of other religions.

Thus, a third characteristic of a sacred text is that it is "classic" in terms of David Tracy's definition: "classics are those texts that have helped found or form a particular culture. . . . that bear an excess and permanence of meaning, yet always resist definitive interpretation."[63] This reminds us of Fishbane's definition of myth, which included the statement that these stories are "constitutive for the founding of a given culture and its rituals." It also hearkens back to my earlier statement that "significant" myths are the ones that keep mattering, that still matter. But most important, Tracy's definition requires that a classic text be open to abundant, even apparently endless interpretation—that it yield ample material for the exegetical imagination. It must not have just one meaning—it "resists definitive interpretation."

Because classic texts have this broad interpretive horizon, they are capable of yielding storied images that reveal Christ to the mythopoet or imaginative exegete. Fishbane's principle of particularity precludes us from constructing a global comparative mythology in which we can claim that every hero or god is "really" Christ. We must respect the particular cultural imagination that produces any given text. This is where historical criticism is

---

62. George Eliot, *Middlemarch*, 2.20.6.
63. Tracy, *Plurality and Ambiguity*, 12.

MYTHOPOESIS

particularly valuable in providing new information to the exegete. A quote from C.S. Lewis on reading medieval poetry applies:

> You can go beyond the first impression that a poem makes on your modern sensibility. By study of things outside the poem, by comparing it with other poems, by steeping yourself in the vanished period, you can then re-enter the poem with eyes more like those of the natives; now perhaps seeing that the associations you gave to the old words were false, that the real implications were different from what you supposed, that what you thought strange was then ordinary and what you thought ordinary was then strange . . . to be led to newer and fresher enjoyments . . . modes of feeling, flavours, atmospheres, nowhere accessible but by a mental journey into the real past.[64]

On the other hand, a classic text with its open interpretive horizon belongs to the world; it matters to us all; and we may borrow its "bricks and beams" in our own mythmaking that bears witness to the one and only Triune God, in the assurance that these new meanings also belong to the text. Thus, even the most startling mythical resonances with the Christian metanarrative—such as the Norse god Odin's self-sacrifice on a tree[65]—do not mean that Odin *is* Christ. Only the particular human Jesus of Nazareth is the Christ, the Son of God. Yet such "good dreams," as C.S. Lewis calls these resonances, are fruitful exegetical material for systematic mythmaking. "These are only a shadow of what is to come, but the substance belongs to Christ."[66]

Such religious resonances also raise the interesting question: to what degree has God used the human imagination—including what we intend for evil[67]—to bring about good? If humans at the dawn of history made sacrifices to God (as in Genesis 4:3–5),

---

64. Lewis, *Studies*, 3.

65. "Odin said: 'I hung from that windswept tree, hung there for nine long nights; I was pierced with a spear; I was an offering to Odin, myself to myself.'" Crossley-Holland, *Norse Myths*, 15.

66. Colossians 2:17.

67. Genesis 50:20.

God "had regard" for their offerings and then allowed sacrifice to remain a central, physical metaphor in atonement and salvation. (See Levenson, *Death and Resurrection of the Beloved Son*, for a fascinating account of a similar theme.) The fullest imagination and fulfillment of atonement "theory" came in the person of Jesus Christ, who *accurately* imagined God, creation, and humankind—and assigned us ultimate significance in his death for us.

MacDonald's favorite term for the mythopoet / skilled interpreter / imaginative exegete was *trouvère*—finder.[68] David Tracy said that "Reality is constituted by the interaction between a text, whether book or world, and a questioning interpreter."[69] In a very real way, the faithful mythopoet is on a constant treasure hunt as she turns up new images that reveal Christ and continually inform her personhood and narrative.

"Misomuthos" ("myth-hater," Tolkien's poetic name for C.S. Lewis before his conversion) once said that myths are lies, even if they are lies breathed through silver. But as dead metaphors, "mere" fictions, or outright lies, myths lose all but aesthetic value. George MacDonald put it this way:

> Let [myth] of mine go for a firefly that now flashes, now is dark, but may flash again. Caught in a hand which does not love its kind, it will turn to an insignificant, ugly thing, that can neither flash nor fly.[70]

---

68. Jeffrey Johnson, "Rooted in All Its Story," 10.

69. Tracy, *Plurality and Ambiguity*, 48.

70. Jeffrey Johnson, "Rooted in All Its Story," 160. Quoted from MacDonald's "The Fantastic Imagination." I have substituted the word "myth" for the original "fairytale."

6

Systematic Mythology

WHILE TOURING A MUSEUM in Naples that mostly featured mosaics from the ruins of Pompeii, I had an unexpected encounter. Turning a corner, I found myself face to face with Artemis of Ephesus. Her arms crawled with lions, her torso was covered in bees and flowers; her face was regal, beautiful. Her bosom was a mass of softly rounded bulbs that almost seemed to sway with life, marble though they were: breasts, bees' butts, or bulls' balls, no one knows for certain.

I think my jaw actually dropped. Artemis was the same goddess whose devotion compelled a city to shout together for two hours: "Great is Artemis of the Ephesians!"[1] What representation of deity is more imaginative than the fantastic, teeming Artemis? How could her significance to the people of Ephesus be more amply demonstrated than that a great crowd should shout with one voice for two hours?

When Paul is touring the Areopagus in Athens, he is "deeply distressed" that the city is full of idols.[2] But he says God has overlooked their ignorance to date, and calls for repentance or "metanoia"—that is, a new mind. A redeemed imagination.

According to George MacDonald:

---

1. Acts 19:34.
2. Acts 17:16–33.

> [W]hile the imagination of man has thus the divine function of putting thought into form, it has a duty altogether human . . . that of following and finding out the divine imagination in whose image it was made. To do this, the man must watch its signs, its manifestations. He must contemplate what the Hebrew poets call the works of His hands.[3]

Jeffrey Johnson says that by this statement, "[MacDonald] was indicating that storied image [including pagan myths] is in and of itself capable of truth-communication, perhaps most especially when its engagement with the Book of Nature is also evident."[4] As the apostle Paul said in his letter to the Romans: "Ever since the creation of the world [God's] eternal power and divine nature, invisible though they are, have been understood and seen through the things he has made."[5]

As for pagan myths, my favorite example is the story of Eros and Psyche, a myth that takes on even greater depth retrospectively following the resurrection of Christ,[6] and one that C.S. Lewis retold in (arguably) his best work (*Till We Have Faces*). The story is an old one that does not belong only to Greek myth; it is reflected in the folktale "Beauty and the Beast" as well as the Norse tale "East of the Sun, West of the Moon" and others. MacDonald says of such stories that "The truer its art, the more things it will mean. . . . [W]hen such forms are new embodiments of Old Truths, we call them products of the Imagination."[7]

As Jeffrey Johnson says, referring to Tolkien, Lewis, and MacDonald's generous use of pagan as well as Christian myth: "To stand in a tradition of Story is both to receive and to be part of 'passing on' that which is infused with the truths of myths that have gone before."[8] C.S. Lewis believed that the medieval mythology

3. MacDonald, *Imagination*, 10.
4. Jeffrey Johnson, "Rooted in All Its Story," 154.
5. Romans 1:20.
6. Jeffrey Johnson, "Rooted in All Its Story," 155.
7. Ibid., 3, quoting MacDonald in "The Fantastic Imagination."
8. Ibid., 18.

surrounding the sun, moon, and five visible planets—a mixture of Greek/Roman myth and Christian cosmology—provided symbols of permanent spiritual value.[9] Here we may also apply the statement of Christ: "Every scribe who has been trained for the kingdom of heaven is like a householder who brings out of his treasure what is new and what is old."[10]

Discussing the idea of a sacred text in light of Ernest Becker's work, Michael Fishbane points out that the Bible provides hints of hope that the "competing symbolic systems" that are "human attempts to live with divinity, and to transcend the specter of death," will ultimately be "neutralized."[11] He locates this hope in Micah's "reinterpretation" (Fishbane's word) of a prophecy from Isaiah:

> [Isaiah] envisioned an era of peace in which all nations would go to Zion to be instructed by the God of Israel (Isa. 2:1–4). The prophet Micah received this tradition intact, but added one revolutionary coda to it: that each nation, Israel included, would go in the name of its own god (Micah 4:5).[12]

In this, Fishbane reads a hope that the Bible may move from being

> . . . a cultural sponsor of raging differences . . . [to become] a prophetic voice [that is] critical of the potential dangers of human symbolic systems, and an advocate for their fragility and plurality. So perceived, the Bible relativizes the idols of the human *textus* for the sake of the divine *textus*; and it points to that sphere where our death is not transcended symbolically, but is absorbed into the fulness of God.[13]

I am not sure what Fishbane means by such absorption, but for a Christian, the meaning is more clear: Our death is not denied

---

9. Ward, *Planet Narnia*, 30.
10. Matthew 13:52 [RSV].
11. Fishbane, *Garments of Torah*, 131.
12. Ibid.
13. Ibid., 131–32.

nor transcended symbolically, but actually transferred to Christ who died for us, and whose resurrection promises eternal life in the New Creation. "All this is from God, who reconciled us to himself through Christ, and has given us the ministry of reconciliation; that is, in Christ God was reconciling the world to himself."[14] "And through him God was pleased to reconcile to himself *all things*, whether on earth or in heaven, by making peace through the blood of his cross."[15] Only in Christ, who is the very image of God and the fullness of the one who fills all in all (τὸ πλήρωμα τοῦ τὰ πάντα ἐν πᾶσιν πληρουμένου),[16] is it possible that the gods of the nations should be taken up into the life of God, reimagined in the image of God, and re-deemed, assigned enduring significance. "People will bring into [the eternal city] the glory and the honor of the nations. But nothing unclean will enter it, nor anyone who practices abomination or falsehood."[17] Only in Christ may the people whose gods are idols—that is, the ungodly—be justified.

Caveats: Where Mythology Fails

Such speculations are fascinating, but we must throw up a few major caveats before being carried any further.

Authority. God, not we, will be the one to choose, or reveal, any such ultimate value assignments. The call to trust in Christ is a call to repentance—to die to the self and to our gods. Only after this death, after being buried in baptism and raised to new life, may we say that whatever beauty we saw in our old gods came from Christ alone. "For all the gods of the peoples are idols, but the LORD made the heavens."[18] Whoever loves his life in this world will lose it; only those who repent, who disregard and even hate the old life and its

14. 2 Corinthians 5:18–19. See also 14, 15.
15. Colossians 1:20.
16. Ephesians 1:23.
17. Revelation 21:26–27.
18. Psalm 96:5.

Systematic Mythology

gods (for the end of those things is death[19]) and trust in Christ as Lord, will see eternal life. Yet if that old life dies—if it is baptized into Christ's death—we are promised that it will bear much fruit.[20] As C.S. Lewis demonstrated so well (narratively) in *The Great Divorce*, "if we insist on keeping [death] (or even earth) we shall not see [Life]: if we accept [Life] we shall not be able to retain even the smallest and most intimate souvenirs of [death].... What [we are] really seeking ... will be there, beyond expectation, waiting for [us] in 'The High Countries.'"[21] "When the true God arrives, then, and only then, 'the half-gods can remain.'"[22]

In the meantime, it is for the Christian to say: "All I once saw as beautiful and significant in my old gods, I now find only—and abounding—in Thee."[23] From that moment, the old myths provide only material—"bricks and beams"—for erecting a new temple to the only God.[24]

Biblical basis. The second caveat is that the word "myth" (μῦθος) occurs only five times in the New Testament, and always in a negative light. Three instances appear in the "pastoral" epistles addressed to Timothy; one in Titus; and one in 2 Peter.[25] Three instances

---

19. Romans 6:21.

20. John 12:24–25.

21. Lewis, *Great Divorce*, 6. I have substituted "death" and "Life" for the original "Hell" and "Heaven," respectively.

22. C.S. Lewis, as quoted in Ward, *Planet Narnia*, 137.

23. Joseph Campbell explains that the "mythic motifs" that are "recurrent themes and features" across religious traditions and "pertain to psychology" were called "'elementary ideas,' *Elementargedanken*," by nineteenth-century apologists at the University of Berlin. (Campbell, *Inner Reaches of Outer Space*, xiii.) This label of *Elementargedanken* bears an interesting resemblance to the στοιχεῖα of the New Testament, translated "elemental spirits" in the NRSV (Galatians 4:3, 9; Colossians 2:8; cf. 2 Peter 3:10). We are absolutely precluded from returning to the service of the elemental spirits or elements once we have "come to know God, or rather to be known by God" (Galatians 4:9).

24. Ephesians 2:21–22: "In him the whole structure is joined together and grows into a holy temple in the Lord; in whom you also are built together spiritually into a dwelling-place for God."

25. 1 Timothy 1:4 and 4:7; 2 Timothy 4:4; Titus 1:14; 2 Peter 1:16.

include adjectives: "godless and silly" myths, "cleverly devised" myths, and "Jewish" myths. We must not ignore these warnings against myths. However, this project does not advocate silly myths nor any story whose focus is not the Triune God. I have defined "myth," not as "fanciful story" which is the primary meaning the UBS dictionary gives for the New Testament usage,[26] but as that narrative world that comprises the individual personhood of every human being, that has as its focus some god, and that is the inevitable result of humanity's meaning-making and imaginative nature. I have also stressed that these personal myths must focus on Christ if they are to reflect ontological or enduring truth—otherwise, they must be either redeemed or discarded.

Subjectivism. Third is the clear danger of rampant subjectivism and moral relativism. As stated earlier, mythmaking is an inevitable activity of human beings, and this is precisely why we must examine our sources and focus. Our myths have effects in the everyday, material world; our imaginations and value assignments affect our neighbors as well as ourselves. Idolatry is not a victimless sin. The use of myth in the Nazi regime is just one of the many sobering examples of myth mismade. Such is the extreme failure to imagine the neighbor in love and to assign him or her the highest significance—and the extreme failure to imagine the God who created, loves, and will judge. The apostle Paul warns:

> **1 Corinthians 3:11–15** [N]o one can lay any foundation other than the one that has been laid; that foundation is Jesus Christ. Now if anyone builds on the foundation with gold, silver, precious stones, wood, hay, straw—the work of each builder will become visible, for the Day will disclose it, because it will be revealed with fire, and the fire will test what sort of work each has done. If what has been built on the foundation survives, the builder will receive a reward. If the work is burned, the builder will suffer loss; the builder will be saved, but only as through fire.

---

26. UBS Concise Dictionary, page 118, in *UBS Greek New Testament*.

Myth versus Materialism

A basic decision for post-postmoderns today is whether to adopt the myth of deism or the myth of materialism. Let us take another look at this question in light of the discussion above.

Physics today is enamored with two postulates: dark matter/energy and the multiverse. Scientists have found that seventy percent of our universe is composed of a mysterious energy that makes galaxies accelerate as the universe expands. They see the effects of this energy, but do not know what it actually is. Similarly, twenty-seven percent of the universe is composed of dark matter. Again, astronomers have detected its effects on the motions of galaxies, but they don't know what it actually is. Both the energy and the matter are called "dark" precisely because we do not know. Meanwhile, most multiverse theories, taken seriously by prominent scientists, hold that there is not one universe but many: that every possible arrangement of matter occurs in some one of the infinite universes that accompany our own in existence. This latter theory has every quality, as C.S. Lewis once said, except that of being useful. There is no explanation here: it claims that *every* possibility is in fact true.

I do not point this out in order to disparage science, which is entirely invaluable and indispensable. But we must not buy into the failed goals of positivism, to think we can either discern or describe the world in an interpretive vacuum.[27] Pure positivism offers no meaning and so far its only answer, its best "theory of everything," is that everything is true—which is no answer at all.

Materialist positivism, then, has no ultimate meaning to offer. From that standpoint, we must all construct our own meaning. From a faith standpoint, it means that the stories we are telling about God are ultimately irrefutable by skeptics; we have as much right to construct meaning as they have. The difference is that we believe there really is a Creator who will re-deem, who will assign our constructions—our identities—with ontological, eternal significance in the living form of Christ.

---

27. The very word "world" is of course an interpretation.

Systematic Mythology

Now with this kind of talk we are once again dancing on the edge of what Murray Rae calls a "mire of subjectivity." Yet he says that "seeing is a belief-laden activity, radically shaped by the personal convictions and perspective of the observer . . . belief *helps us to see*. . . . [The biblical worldview] constitutes the foundations of a construal of the world . . . in which God as creator brings the world into being . . . and is engaged throughout history in bringing the world to its fulfilment in loving communion with himself."[28]

The materialist viewpoint is no doubt one of the major sources of today's moral relativism and therapeutic deism.[29] It seems to indicate that everyone's personal story is true for them, which is indeed the shared belief of my generation. But as I described at length above, the natural (fallen) human imagination objectifies and kills the living and pretends the dead is alive. It mislocates significance and elevates preliminary concerns to the status of ultimate concern.[30] In short, we produce and worship idols. The tale we are telling must not ultimately be about the self. The god in our innermost temple must die, and we must be occupied—saved—by the living Christ.[31]

Living Myth

One of the opening quotes of this project was the question of Jesus Christ in Matthew 22:20: "Τίνος ἡ εἰκὼν αὕτη καὶ ἡ ἐπιγραφή;" That is: "Whose image and inscription is this?" Christ was asking about a coin, but he also asks this question of each one of us. That which we cling to and trust above all things—our ultimate

---

28. Rae, *History and Hermeneutics*, 97.

29. For a full treatment of the current generation's reliance on subjectivity and moral therapeutic deism, see Smith and Snell, *Souls in Transition*. See also comedian Stephen Colbert's useful (and facetious) term "truthiness"—that which has the quality of being what I want to believe, such that reference to facts is unnecessary.

30. Tillich, *Systematic Theology*, 13. "Idolatry is the elevation of a preliminary concern to ultimacy."

31. A new *numen* in the ναός of our νοῦς.

concern—is our god.[32] The narrative world we are each constructing has as its focus some god: we are becoming conformed to that image, and we are shaping our lives according to that story. Whose image is it, and whose inscription[33]—whose tale?

> Jeremiah 31:33–34 [Thus says] the LORD: I will put my *torah* [instruction] within them, and I will write it on their hearts; and I will be their God, and they shall be my people. No longer shall they teach one another, or say to each other, "Know the LORD," for they shall all know me, from the least of them to the greatest, says the LORD.

Fishbane says that "Myth may . . . comprise and condition a mystical mentality—not by being transcended so much as by being fully subjectivized and lived. . . . [T]he images of myth constitute an interior landscape of the soul by which they may, in truth, conform to the reality of God."[34] Brevard Childs adds: "Whereas the man of critical mind thinks of the world about him as passive and impersonal, the primitive [sic] man conceives of his surroundings as active and living, with powers which influence every area of his life."[35] The Christian conceives of those powers as subject, finally, to one Power: the Almighty Creator and Redeemer, the Triune God, the Lord.

Mythmaking works both ways. Our world has a divine Author, a Creator Mythopoet. Myths are significant to God because they are one of the means by which God mediates God's relationship with humanity and each individual. They are imaginative because God's work of creation invests the eternal, invisible Word into the unformed material of the cosmos, and particularly into

---

32. See Luther's explication of the first commandment in the Large Catechism, Kolb et al., *Book of Concord*, 386–92. "To have a God . . . is nothing else than to trust yourself to him completely," including your "whole heart and confidence" (388).

33. If Ricoeur is correct that inscription means "the author's intention and the meaning of the text cease to coincide," what that might mean for a human so inscribed by God? (Ricoeur, *Interpretation Theory*, 30.)

34. Fishbane, *Biblical Myth*, 314.

35. Childs, *Myth and Reality*, 17.

human individuals, forming images out of what began as the raw ground of existence made visible by the Spirit's power.

Despite our self-destructive ways, God will not allow us to return everything back to nothing.[36] But this is no mere rescue: God "chose us in Christ before the foundation of the world."[37] "My Father is still working, and I also am working."[38] God continues to *create*, to enrich God's own life with new meaning, in the same sense in which the prodigal son's family was "enriched" by his adventures.[39] We are called to participate in the work of reimagining this world as an informed substance; to share the good news that Jesus Christ is Lord and to work against the powers that objectify; to reimagine the world as a garden rather than a grave. To consciously and creatively become a part of the story God is telling, a story in which Christ is all, and in all.

Enacted Exegesis

Hans Georg Gadamer, Paul Ricoeur, and others have demonstrated that the meaning of a text is not limited to the intention of its author nor to the interpretation of any one reader. As described earlier, this is especially true of inspired and classic texts. Kirstin Jeffrey Johnson describes George MacDonald's experience of this truth:

> MacDonald was acutely aware of the challenge ambiguity of language brought even to Scripture. He discovered

---

36. Athanasius, *On the Incarnation*, 31–32 (§6). "Man, who was created in God's image . . . was disappearing. . . . The thing that was happening was in truth both monstrous and unfitting . . . that beings which once had shared the nature of the Word should perish and turn back again into non-existence through corruption . . . that the work of God . . . should disappear. . . . It was impossible, therefore, that God should leave man to be carried off by corruption, because it would be unfitting and unworthy of Himself."

37. Ephesians 1:4.

38. John 5:17.

39. Thanks to Duane Priebe for this idea, which is his personal recollection of a statement by René Dubos in a discussion at a Nobel Conference at Gustavus Adolphus College, 1977.

Systematic Mythology

in his own struggles with translation—especially in Scots, German, Greek, and Hebrew in particular—that it is impossible to carry all context of one word over into a world of a whole other language, for each function within a particular context. . . . [H]e saw [this as] a gift of richness proffered in truths designed to meet ever-changing contexts.[40]

Later in her thesis, she continues: "Each word can carry with it a myriad of overtones, allusions, and insinuations; language is polysemous. Particular phrases are embedded with histories. Yet despite the accompanying challenges, MacDonald—as Tolkien, Lewis, and Barfield—delights in multiplicity of meanings and ever deepening intertextual dialogue."[41] This dialogue is not only a conversation between mythopoet and source texts; the reader— the "friend"[42]—is also involved in the development of meaning. "Intertextuality is an observation of relationships between texts that places the generation of meaning in the dynamic conversation between text/intertext/reader."[43] Particular phrases are embedded with histories, language is polysemous, in part because readers are particular, concrete individuals with histories, relationships, and language of their own.[44] Indeed, any person—any self—may be

---

40. Jeffrey Johnson, "Rooted in All Its Story," 51.

41. Ibid., 179.

42. I am referring to the MacDonald quote from the "Giving Form to Thought" section above: "How shall the one show the other that which is invisible? . . . [H]e seizes [a] symbol, as the garment or body of his invisible thought, presents it to his friend, and his friend understands him." MacDonald, *Imagination*, 8.

43. Giere, *New Glimpse of Day One*, 3.

44. "[E]very single brain is absolutely individual, both in its development and in the way it encounters the world. Your brain develops depending on your individual history. What has gone on in your own brain and its consciousness over your lifetime is not repeatable, ever—not with identical twins, not even with conjoined twins. Each brain is exposed to different circumstances. It's very likely that your brain is unique in the history of the universe." Kruglinski, "What Makes You Uniquely 'You'?," para. 5.

Systematic Mythology

defined as the center of a unique pattern of relationships.[45] That includes each person's particular narrative.

Through these many layers of meaning, Jeffrey Johnson says, MacDonald's mythopoesis approaches the Subject of all his story. By masterfully combining language, intertextual dialogue, relationship, a keen engagement with his world, context, Scripture, and stories that have gone before into the medium of narrative, MacDonald "exerts a power" that

> beholds the work and its Creator, things seen and things unseen. . . . He looks directly and always into the soul of things, and that soul is to him the immanent God. The Divine omnipresence, as a dogma, we all believe; with him it is more than a belief—a perception, a face-to-face communion. We are afraid to associate the Divine image with paltry things, with every-day affairs, with trivial needs, vexations, and enjoyments; to him the least things seem great, because he sees God in them.[46]

Seeing the world in this way is certainly the work of the religious imagination. It systematically associates each particularity of one's context with the Divine Subject of our story; taking every thought captive. This is what I am calling systematic mythology; it may also be called a sacramental worldview.[47]

As Jeffrey Johnson puts it, "[MacDonald's] 'theology' is his holistic worldview—his *Weltanschauung*—incorporating culture, language, environment, ethos, and community, all in relation to God."[48] And again, "[T]hat word and Word, light and Light, mythic god of Truest Myth transcended time, space, and sense, so that

---

45. Thanks to Duane Priebe for this indispensable idea. It was beautifully expanded by the writer Charles Mudede: "A biological point processed in time and through space; a point at which the lines from multiple directions and distances (the light from a star, the words from lips) arrive, intersect, and concentrate."

46. MacDonald, *Imagination*, 4, from the introduction by A.P. Peabody.

47. C.S. Lewis said: "The attempt to read [the invisible world] through its sensible imitations, to see the archetype in the copy, is what I mean by symbolism or sacramentalism." Ward, *Planet Narnia*, 30.

48. Jeffrey Johnson, "Rooted in All Its Story," xxiv.

Systematic Mythology

any person might apprehend the most important revelation. The sacramental does not recognize a division between earthy and holy: earthiness is holiness, by definition of the Creator's own act."[49] The end goal is not only to behold God, but to be transformed in relationship. As Jeffrey Johnson says: "Such is the model of the Incarnate Story through whom all Creation is transformed; enacted exegesis in sympathy with the heart of the Author."[50]

Each one of us has the opportunity to constantly inform our substance through personal practices of reading and charity as well as ritual, that is, gathering together.[51] The worship practices, the liturgy, of the church are abstracted (exegeted) from Scripture and, like the creeds, have stood the test of time. They continue to matter to us as a material expression of our mythology; as Eliseo Vivas describes it, "[God] is apprehended as a tremendous mystery, in relation to which we recognize ourselves as creatures. A complex and strong affectivity is elicited . . . when our response is fresh. . . . Liturgy is intended to keep, and often does keep, the response fresh."[52]

Our cultic activities—for that is what liturgy really is—are the expression, ever new, of our mythology. Each repetition of the doxology brings fresh glory to God; each psalm manifests God in a new way whenever it is "mattered" within a particular congregation of particular, concrete individuals. The sacrament lets us taste and see that God is good. In this way, the world is constantly informed, constantly imagined in terms of Christ. In this way, we live, move, and have our being in a narrative and physical world that grows as a rich and tangled garden of myth and symbol, planted (like Eden) by God. We perceive bright filaments of myth wrapped around every tree, thorn, and cup; every good and perfect gift we recognize as coming direct from the living hand of our God. We are grasped by the logos,[53] formed in an image, loved and created,

---

49. Ibid., 239.
50. Ibid., 246.
51. Hebrews 10:25.
52. Vivas, "Myth," 349.
53. To invert Tillich's language (Tillich, *Systematic Theology*, 75).

taken captive and set free. This is the "faithful performance"[54] that makes God's story visible; it is "enacted exegesis in sympathy with the heart of the Author."[55]

The Author of All Our Story

God is indeed the ultimate and only Author of life and the story of this world. Yet systematic mythology suggests that God has chosen to tell that story, not by dictation, but by multiplication. God has populated our world with creatures who are skilled interpreters, who tell individual and cultural stories, who assign significance and imaginatively combine the visible and invisible. "[We] may actually assist in the effoliation and multiple enrichment of creation. All tales may come true; and yet, at the last, redeemed, they may be as like and unlike the forms that we give them as [humans], finally redeemed, will be like and unlike the fallen that we know."[56]

Our natural, fallen exegesis mislocates significance and imagines (and worships) things that are dead. But God so loved the world that God sent Jesus Christ to save the world: to make our death like his and our resurrection like his,[57] to justify the ungodly, and to redeem out of our poor attempts at storytelling a New Creation that abounds in multiplied meaning, that manifests the image of Christ in billions of redeemed faces, that tells the story of "what God has done" in billions of particular tales. That is filled with all the fullness of God.[58]

God has "devised a plan" to redeem our life. We are caught in a hand that loves our kind!

Thus, the gospel is an invitation to embrace the story of Christ—who lived, died, rose again, and is Lord of all—as the comprehensive rubric for imagining our God, ourselves, and our

54. Hart and Guthrie, *Faithful Performances*.
55. Jeffrey Johnson, "Rooted in All Its Story," 246.
56. Tolkien, *Tree and Leaf*, 73.
57. Romans 6:5.
58. Mannermaa, *Christ Present in Faith*, 21, 45.

Systematic Mythology

reality. But the call to enter this narrative is not a safe, hedge-your-bets kind of call. It's not just an alternate story to the materialist one, a constructed narrative that is more pleasant to live. God's hand is not a "safe" place to be.[59] Instead, it is a call to discipleship: a call to come and die. Our hero and god is one who was crucified, and who calls us to take up our own crosses. Christ took up our death, but in the process, he claimed our life.

When we "cultivate full renunciation" and "make a gift of ourselves to the highest powers," it is really that: giving ourselves away, becoming a living sacrifice to God.[60] Bultmann said that "Myth is ... an expression of man's awareness that he is not lord of his own being. It expresses his sense of dependence not only within the visible world, but more especially on those forces which hold sway beyond the confines of the known.... To believe means not to have apprehended but to have been apprehended."[61] If myth reminds us that we are not lord of our own being, systematic mythology tells us that indeed we have a sovereign Lord and god—and more than a hero—a master and judge.

Earlier we noted that a worldview changes only when the old one becomes untenable. Dan Olson describes this as a crisis: a situation from which you *cannot* emerge as the same person. The word *crisis* comes from the Greek word for judgment. When systematic mythology considers God's judgment, it is the identity that hangs in the balance. It's not a simple question of right and wrong. Who will you be?

The word "doom" originally meant judgment, not some long-determined fate. A judge would pronounce a doom, or verdict. When we consider the value of something, we "deem" it.

God judges in light of Christ. Those who participate in Christ's own life and righteousness by faith[62] are re-deemed, their stories assumed into the fullness of God,[63] their value

---

59. Ecclesiastes 9:1.
60. Romans 12:1.
61. Bultmann, *Kerygma and Myth*, 11, 21.
62. Mannermaa, *Christ Present in Faith*, xii, 2, 7, 16, 29, 44–45.
63. Ibid., 21, 45.

assignments informing the reality of creation. Indeed, they have a new doom: they are conformed to the image of Christ. Justified, the ungodly become gods.

The Crucified God

As the hymn says: "Tell me the old, old story of unseen things above; of Jesus and his glory; of Jesus and his love." Our God is the crucified God, the one who loved us, bore our sin, and died for us. Earlier we discussed the work of Ernest Becker and the fact that we cannot be the hero of our own myth if we wish to avoid neurosis, despair, and ultimate meaninglessness. According to Becker, "If you are going to be a hero then you must give a gift."[64] Only one human in all of history was able to give himself completely to "the highest powers," that is, to God; only one human is able to bear the burden of determining our ultimate concern, to be our hero, to be our justification: to "grant the immortality of [our] personal soul."[65]

> **Philippians 2:5-11** Let the same mind be in you that was in Christ Jesus, who, though he was in the form of God, did not regard equality with God as something to be exploited, but emptied himself, taking the form of a slave, being born in human likeness. And being found in human form, he humbled himself and became obedient to the point of death—even death on a cross. Therefore God also highly exalted him and gave him the name that is above every name, so that at the name of Jesus every knee should bend, in heaven and on earth and under the earth, and every tongue should confess that Jesus Christ is Lord, to the glory of God the Father.

In his death, Christ justified the ungodly claim that God is dead, and that we have killed him.[66] "Christian theology can use

---

64. Becker, *Denial of Death*, 173.

65. Ibid.

66. An idea explored by Hegel, Heidegger, and others, and made famous by Nietzsche.

the word 'God' meaningfully only in a context which is defined by the understanding of the human person Jesus . . . we must always remember that this man was *crucified*, that he was killed. . . . [T]he Crucified One is . . . the real definition of what is meant with the word 'God.'"[67] And yet in the resurrection of Jesus, God declared him to be Lord of all[68] and granted to him the life of every creature who trusts in him. Thus, in Christ, God took up ("assumed") the whole of humanity's life in all its forms and cultures—including the full range of creaturely religious imagination—into the life of God, redeeming and reconciling the world.

> **Colossians 1:15-20** He is the image of the invisible God, the firstborn of all creation; for in him all things in heaven and on earth were created, things visible and invisible, whether thrones or dominions or rulers or powers—all things have been created through him and for him. He himself is before all things, and in him all things hold together. He is the head of the body, the church; he is the beginning, the firstborn from the dead, so that he might come to have first place in everything. For in him all the fullness of God was pleased to dwell, and through him God was pleased to reconcile to himself all things, whether on earth or in heaven, by making peace through the blood of his cross.

Practice

Systematic mythology offers at least two practical recommendations.

Study Scripture. The Bible is the primary text for interpreting the world; it should be the foundational exegetical source that forms and troubles all our mythmaking. Dan Olson has said: "As Christians, we are called to make sense of life using Scripture as a lens for seeing the whole of reality." Colossians 3:16a admonishes: "Let the word of Christ dwell in you richly." What might that mean,

---

67. Jüngel, *God as the Mystery of the World*, 12-13.
68. Romans 1:4 and Philippians 2:9-11.

except to refer constantly to your god and hero in your daily life and to constantly inform your mind with God's inspired Word? Scripture is the essential and trustworthy text for our imaginative exegesis guided by the Spirit. We are not left alone in this world; the Spirit is with us to guide us into all truth.[69]

Like Abraham, persevere as though you see the one who is invisible.[70] The more you inform your mind with Scripture, the more you signify and imagine your narrative world as the story of Christ, the richer you will find that world and the more visible your God. You yourself will begin to reflect the image of your Creator as you are renewed in knowledge:

> **Colossians 3:5–17** [RSV] Put to death therefore what is earthly in you: fornication, impurity, passion, evil desire, and covetousness, which is idolatry. . . . In these you once walked, when you lived in them. . . . [But now] you have put off the old nature with its practices and have put on the new nature, which is being renewed in knowledge after the image of its creator. . . . Let the word of Christ dwell in you richly, teach and admonish one another in all wisdom, and sing psalms and hymns and spiritual songs with thankfulness in your hearts to God. And whatever you do, in word or deed, do everything in the name of the Lord Jesus, giving thanks to God the Father through him.

Interpret your neighbor charitably. This includes her image, her motives, and her story. Remember that the proper work of imagination is love. Keep in mind that the significance of every other human was declared once for all when Christ died for that person.[71] Do not judge or objectify; remember that "Life is the process

---

69. John 16:13.

70. Hebrews 11:27.

71. This also fulfills the eighth commandment as explicated by Luther in the Small Catechism: "You are not to bear false witness against your neighbor. . . . We are to fear and love God, so that we do not tell lies about our neighbors, betray or slander them, or destroy their reputations. Instead we are to come to their defense, speak well of them, and interpret everything they do

in which potential being becomes actual being."[72] Walking in the Spirit means imagining your neighbor in the way that gives the most life.[73] As McAdams said, "the most mature personal myths are those that enhance the mythmaking of others."[74] Our personal mythologies lack a critical aspect—they reflect a failure of imagination—if they do not move us to good works of ministry and self-sacrifice in imitation of and in gratitude to our Lord and as a means of living out God's love for the world.

Conclusion

This project has explored three primary questions.

1. **What is a myth?** Answer: An imaginative articulation or narrative that relates to our ultimate concern—our God—in visible terms. It constitutes and interprets both our world and identity.

2. **How do we make myths (that is, meaning)?** By imaginatively exegeting sacred texts. Yet we consistently imagine things that are dead, we objectify our neighbors, and we assign ultimate significance to preliminary concerns (idols). Only in Christ and his work are our idolatry and death redeemed and resurrected.

3. **What does this mean for a post-Enlightenment, postmodern individual?** The mythical language in Scripture provides a rich and trustworthy source of exegetical material for faithful devotional practice and personal mythmaking. Both science and poetry are essential;

---

in the best possible light." Kolb et al., *Book of Concord*, 353.

72. Tillich, *Systematic Theology*, 241.

73. "If [you] are spiritual . . . do what characterizes spiritual people. . . . What else does it mean to be spiritual than to be a child of the Holy Spirit and to have the Holy Spirit? But the Holy Spirit is the Paraclete, the Advocate, the Comforter. . . . He excuses, extenuates, and completely covers our sins. On the other hand, He magnifies our faith and good works. Those who imitate Him . . . with regard to the sins of their fellowmen are spiritual." Luther, *Luther's Works*, 389.

74. McAdams, *Stories We Live By*, 113.

Systematic Mythology

we need not rely on materialist positivism to reveal the significance of the world. Instead, the fullness of truth is found and redeemed in Christ, the Living Word who is (in the abundance of his incarnation) both *logos* and *mythos*. We are called to participate in the myth of the crucified god—including creation, redemption, and the hope of the resurrection—imaginatively and charitably informing or signifying our world until the earth is "filled with the knowledge of the glory of the Lord, as the waters cover the sea."[75]

The baptized imagination brings everything subject to Christ, including our life, identity, and insecurities; our neighbors; and our world. "[T]he love of Christ controls [or constrains] us, because we are convinced that one has died for all."[76] "When he ascended on high, he made captivity itself a captive; he gave gifts to his people."[77] "We take every thought captive to obey Christ."[78]

George MacDonald said that Christ suffered and died, not so that we should not suffer or die, but so that our suffering and death would be like his.[79] Death is not only our greatest fear—the threat of ultimate meaninglessness—but also poses a threat to God's work of creation.[80] In Christ, God has taken that death up into God's own life and overcome it. God has assumed all our particular forms of brokenness—all our failures of imagination and misplaced significance—and has justified the ungodly. All that is left is for us to respond in trust: to "love the truth and so be saved."[81] "[I]f we have been united with him in a death like his, we will certainly be united with him in a resurrection like his."[82] Then we will know

---

75. Habakkuk 2:14.
76. 2 Corinthians 5:14 [RSV].
77. Ephesians 4:8.
78. 2 Corinthians 10:5b.
79. Opening quote for Lewis, *Problem of Pain*. Attributed to "Unspoken Sermons. First Series."
80. Athanasius, *On the Incarnation*, 31–32 (§6). See note 36 on page 78.
81. 2 Thessalonians 2:10b.
82. Romans 6:5.

fully, just as we are fully known; then we will see God face to face.[83] This is the incredible hope of the Christian myth.

> **Isaiah 26:19** [RSV] Thy dead shall live, their bodies shall rise. O dwellers in the dust, awake and sing for joy! For thy dew is a dew of light, and on the land of the shades thou wilt let it fall.

---

83. 1 Corinthians 13:12.

Afterword: A Blessing

READER, THANK YOU FOR your time and charitable attention. I leave you with a blessing from George MacDonald:

> May the God of peace give you peace.
> May the love of Christ constrain you.
> May the gifts of the Holy Spirit be yours.[1]

Or in terms of systematic mythology: May God grasp your right hand and focus your imagination upon God's self, making invisible those fears and anxieties that clamor to be your idols. May love for Christ be your first and highest love; may he hold your imagination captive; may Christ give you his own forgiving, self-sacrificing, justifying, divinizing love and teach you to focus that love upon your neighbors and yourself. May the power of the Holy Spirit to unite, realize, and manifest the visible and invisible and conform it to the image of Christ be the power you bring to your life and world, every day and in every detail.

Amen.

---

1. MacDonald, *Imagination*, 297.

Appendix

And All the Tribes Fear Him

This essay was written for a Festschrift to honor Duane A. Priebe, professor of systematic theology at Wartburg Theological Seminary. It was originally published in Currents in Theology and Mission, *Vol. 41, No. 1.*

THE INSIDE PASSAGE OF the Pacific Northwest—the waterway from Seattle to Alaska—is a place of mountains and sea, islands and surf and eagles, whales and canoes and fantastic art. Its gardens are tangles of thorny rosebushes and delicate ferns, made radiant by the setting sun whose light is thrown up again and again from deep seawater. Here one eats salmon and clams outdoors among tall and fragrant cedars, and listens for the wingbeats of the Thunderbird—that mighty avian that hunts whales, stunning them with the twin Lightning Snakes that live under its wings, and carrying them off to the skyscraping mountain peaks to feast.[1] But if you do not glimpse the Thunderbird, then at least you can hope to catch sight of a tiny golden hummingbird sipping eagerly from a thicket of fuchsia.

Somewhere in this verdant seascape, near the Queen Charlotte Strait in the late nineteenth century, a Kwakwaka'wakw artist carved a model totem pole. With the influx of European traders had come many new complications, among them Christianity and disease, but also new pigments and an eager market for the indigenous art, which was unlike anything the rest of the world had

---

1. Hilary Stewart, *Looking at Indian Art of the Northwest Coast* (University of Washington Press, 2003).

APPENDICES: APPLIED MYTHOLOGY

seen. The coastal tribes' towering totem poles, tremendous cedar logs carved with the highly stylized images of a family's crest and heritage and raised to commemorate their potlatch feasts, truly evoked that old metaphor: they captured the imagination. They still do. To meet the sudden demand for their highly unique art, enterprising indigenous sculptors created "model" totem poles: smaller versions of their titanic originals, suitable for tourists to purchase and carry away.

Kwakwaka'wakw (Kwakiutl) model totem pole, red cedar, late nineteenth century. Collection of Cornelia Duryée. Photo by Paul Macapia. Courtesy Seattle Art Museum. Printed by permission.

Our artist chose to create a model totem pole in the distinctive sculptural style of the Kwakwaka'wakw people, but with the unusual subject of a nursing mother at the top, seated on a sea monster. The other characters (in descending order) included a wolf, an octopus, and a man. In addition to traditional black, the model was painted with ultramarine and vermilion, non-local pigments available only through trade with Europeans.[2]

Authors Aldona Jonaitis and Aaron Glass describe the history of the totem pole as "a history of colonial relations, for it emerged . . . in the context of transactions between the original inhabitants of and the newcomers to the Northwest Coast."[3] This is especially true of model totem poles, which were essentially created as souvenirs. They serve as "significant documents of the intercultural encounter. Carvers understood and took advantage of the ready market for these items, which they knew would travel . . . to territories remote from their own, by people who had little understanding of the subtleties of their artistic and cultural heritage."[4] As souvenirs, the models did little to educate their new owners about the deeper cultural realities of indigenous artists, but instead became the locus of personal memories and the embodiment of assigned meanings; outsiders subjected both models and full-size totem poles to "varied judgments, intepretations, appropriations, or celebrations, and in the process imposed on the artworks meanings that their Native creators could never have imagined."[5]

A Text in a New Context

Many years later, the model totem pole was photographed for a book called *The Box of Daylight*, edited by the art historian Bill Holm, who first undertook to formally analyze the unique

---

2. Photo and description are from Bill Holm, *The Box of Daylight: Northwest Coast Indian Art* (University of Washington Press, 1983), 114.

3. Aldona Jonaitis and Aaron Glass, *The Totem Pole: An Intercultural History* (University of Washington Press, 2010), 9.

4. Ibid., 103.

5. Ibid., 9.

characteristics of Northwest Coast art.[6] The book is filled with samples of all the power and splendor of the coastal tribes' artistic vision, with its refracted forms and ovoid shapes that seem to capture the essence of life as reflected in seawater, and of a mythical understanding that all the animals used to be people.[7]

This model totem pole in particular captured my imagination because it features a nursing mother seated on a sea monster—two images that are evocative for most if not all the human race. And for anyone who has studied the biblical accounts of creation with Dr. Duane Priebe, the words "sea monster" immediately conjure conflict mythology—the development or ordering of the world via divine battle with a sea monster.

But does the sea monster of Kwakwaka'wakw mythology bear any resemblance to the sea monster of the Bible and its role in the ancient Israelite creation accounts?

The Sea Monster in Kwakwaka'wakw Tradition

The Kwakwaka'wakw sea monster goes by several names: Tseygis,[8] Yagis,[9] Yakim. (The last name means "badness."[10]) One of the many fabulous denizens of Kwakwaka'wakw religion, art, and mythology, the sea monster makes his appearance at their winter ceremonies in the form of a mask, or may appear as a primary totem of a family, as it does in Chief John Scow's "Sea Monster house," erected around 1900 to honor the family crest of the 'Namgis

---

6. Not to be confused with the poet and travel writer Bill Holm who often focused on Iceland.

7. Dr. Jessica Joyce Christie, ed., *Landscapes of Origin in the Americas: Creation Narratives Linking Ancient Places and Present Communities* (University of Alabama Press, 2009), 45.

8. Holm, *The Box of Daylight*, 114.

9. Personal correspondence with Bill Holm, May 2013.

10. Wayne Suttles and William Sturtevant, eds., *Handbook of North American Indians, Volume 7: Northwest Coast* (Smithsonian Institution Scholarly Press, 1990), 375. The article continues: "Masks portraying Iakim take many forms, as all versions of sea monsters are called by this term."

tribe.[11] Supernatural beings or "numaym" like the sea monster are the founding members of a given group or family; the traditions are carefully preserved, as they govern various family privileges and status.[12]

The monster's home is the undersea world, which is associated with food (fish) and riches (copper). One of his distinctive features is a wide, gaping mouth.[13] Like the Thunderbird or the Sisiyutl (a double-headed snake with a grinning human face at its center), the sea monster is eerie or "wonderful," distinct from any merely natural creature. He "obstructs rivers, endangers lakes and the sea, and swallows and upsets canoes. The sea is said to boil when he rises, and all the tribes fear him."[14]

> He makes the deep boil like a pot; he makes the sea like a pot of ointment.
>
> He leaves a shining wake behind him; one would think the deep to be white-haired.
>
> On earth he has no equal, a creature without fear.
>
> No one is so fierce as to dare to stir him up. Who can stand before him?
>
> Job 41:31–33, 10

More specific references to the sea monster are tantalizing and few, slippery as fish. The monster arises where there are reefs.[15] Sometimes it is described as having the shape of a halibut, possibly with humans standing along its edge. In connection

---

11. "Chief Scow's House," Bill Reid Centre for Northwest Coast Art Studies, Simon Fraser University. http://www.sfu.ca/brc/virtual_village/Kwakwaka_wakw/gwayasdums--gilford-island-/chief-scow-s-house.html.

12. Suttles and Sturtevant, *Handbook of North American Indians, Volume 7*, 373.

13. Personal correspondence with Bill Holm, May 2013.

14. Suttles and Sturtevant, *Handbook of North American Indians, Volume 7*, 375.

15. Franz Boas, *The Religion of the Kwakiutl Indians: Texts* (Columbia University Press, 1930), 178. Note that the term "Kwakiutl" is no longer in widespread use. It was replaced by the term favored by the tribes: Kwakwaka'wakw.

with the world deluge story, which is common among Native Americans, it is said that:

> One ancestor of the 'Namgis Tribe was sent a message from the Creator in a dream that when the flood came, the great halibut-like Sea Monster 'Namxiyalagiyu "Only One" would rise from the depths of the ocean and take him to a place where he would be protected for the duration of the flood.... This creature was so big that the man appeared to be a small speck on the rim of the monster.[16]

The man is given the ability to breathe underwater and is taken by the monster to a safe place under the sea until the floods finally abate. The monster then returns him to dry land. In some versions, a family is vomited up by the sea monster and revived by the Creator.[17]

> *But the LORD provided a large fish to swallow up Jonah; and Jonah was in the belly of the fish for three days and three nights. . . . Then the LORD spoke to the fish, and it spewed Jonah out upon the dry land.*
>
> Jonah 1:17; 2:10

As a *numaym*, the Kwakwaka'wakw sea monster makes his most frequent appearance at their winter ceremonies, elaborate rituals that not only celebrated various family totems, but also did the important work of taming the cannibal dancer who must be restored to his humanity. The Kwakwaka'wakw's highly developed "dramatic arts cannot be separated from the potlatch,"[18] feasts in which material goods were lavished upon attendees to the honor of the host. The greatest potlatches were those "to which 'all the tribes' were invited."[19]

---

16. Christie, *Landscapes of Origin in the Americas*, 45.

17. Boas, *The Religion of the Kwakiutl Indians*, 178.

18. Suttles and Sturtevant, *Handbook of North American Indians, Volume 7*, 379.

19. Ibid., 372.

Chaos and Creation

In the Hebrew Bible, sea monsters are closely connected with the idea of creation. For example, speaking of Psalm 74 (see especially verses 12–17), Jon Levenson explains that "the context is . . . one of creation, provided we do not restrict our understanding of the term to the traditional, but postbiblical, doctrine of *creatio ex nihilo*."[20] In Psalm 104, that great paean to God's world, Leviathan sports in the sea. In Job, where God overwhelms the innocent sufferer by recounting the wonders and mighty aspects of the creative work, the Leviathan is a prominent figure. In the world deluge story, which is a kind of second creation,[21] God opens the fountains of the great deep (*tehom*) as well as the windows of heaven—letting the waters above the sky spill down onto the earth. And why were there waters above the sky? In the Enuma Elish, when Marduk used a fierce wind to inflate and overcome the water monster goddess Tiamat, "he split her in half to form the sky and the Earth."[22] Echoes of this worldview remained even when Tiamat had been ungodded. Indeed, she is even referenced (in a whisper) in Genesis 1 with that word *tehom*, "the Deep," and in Psalm 148: "sea monsters and all deeps."

Scholar Safwat Marzouk describes this theme:

> Various ancient Near Eastern *Chaoskampf* myths (e.g., Enuma Elish, Baal Cycle, Re-Apophis) speak of the concept of chaos (e.g., political, natural, etc.) as an embodied entity, as a monster. Tiamat, Yamm, Mot, and Apophis, who represent chaos in Enuma Elish, Baal Cycle, and Re-Apophis respectively, are embodied. Though on the surface chaos seems gigantic and out of control, the purpose of the combat myth is to assure the reader that this chaos is contained and will eventually be defeated.[23]

---

20. Jon D. Levenson, *Creation and the Persistence of Evil: The Jewish Drama of Divine Omnipotence* (Princeton, N.J.: Princeton University Press, 1994), 9.

21. "[T]he story of Noah and his survival of the great deluge is a reiteration of primordial creation." Ibid., 73.

22. Ibid., 121.

23. Safwat Marzouk, paper presented to the Society of Biblical Literature:

APPENDICES: APPLIED MYTHOLOGY

If the ancient Israelites feared the sea and associated it with chaos, the Northwest Coast tribes loved the sea because it was their abundant source of food, society, and wealth.[24] And yet, even the sea-loving Kwakwaka'wakw might be peacefully floating about in a canoe when something monstrous could explode out of the depths with overwhelming power.

Cosmogony and Liturgy

Franz Boas, a primary anthropologist of the Kwakwaka'wakw, makes it clear that the coastal tribes do not have an *ex nihilo* origin myth such as the Western tradition presumes:

> The idea of creation, in the sense of a projection into objective existence of a world that pre-existed in the mind of a creator, is ... almost entirely foreign to the American race. ... There was no unorganized chaos preceding the origin of the world. Everything has always been in existence in objective form somewhere.[25]

And yet, as one scholar argues:

> [T]he ultimate aim of pre-colonial Kwakwaka'wakw cosmology was the regeneration of the natural world ... Kwakwaka'wakw ritual forms [were] aspects of a cosmogonic scheme ... the Kwakwaka'wakw saw themselves as participants in a universal ecology requiring continuous maintenance.[26]

"The Semiotics of the Dismembered Body of the Monster in the ANE Chaoskampf Myths and Ezekiel in the Light of Foucault's Discipline and Punish," November 2012, Chicago.

24. Suttles and Sturtevant, *Handbook of North American Indians*, Volume 7, 364.

25. Franz Boas, *Race, Language, and Culture* (University of Chicago Press, 1995), 468.

26. "'It Is a Strict Law That Bids Us Dance': Cosmologies, Colonialism, Death, and Ritual Authority in the Kwakwaka'wakw Potlatch, 1849 to 1922," Joseph Masco, Comparative Studies in Society and History, Vol. 37, No. 1 (January 1995), 44–46.

The elaborate Kwakwaka'wakw winter ceremonies were essential for maintaining—and thus creating—the world. As with the Enuma Elish, and later in Israelite liturgy, chaos could be neutralized in cult. Jon Levenson explains:

> [T]he creative ordering of the world has become something that humanity can not only witness and celebrate, but something in which it can also take part . . . through the cult . . . we are enabled to cope with evil, for it is the cult that builds and maintains order, transforms chaos into creation.[27]

Such ritual mythology can reveal the essential outlook of the human condition: Sin as the fearful, ravening cannibal that wants to devour rather than serve its neighbor. Monsters rising all unexpected from the depths, causing the sea to boil in a hoary swath of chaos. Regular gatherings and rituals, the community performances that are so essential to keeping our "world" going.

This human situation is not incidental. The doctrine of the Incarnation demands that we take the nature of humanity seriously, including its imaginative life. As Duane Priebe has said:

> What God has done in Christ can be understood only in the context of the history of the entire world and its cultures. Conversely, he is the whole through whom our world, cultures and histories come into their truth.[28]

Just as all the tribes are invited to the greatest potlatches in which wealth is reckoned in terms of what is given away and the cannibal is finally tamed, so all the world is invited to Christ's triumphant feast in which he shares his own body and blood and the glory of his resurrection.

---

27. Levenson, *Creation and the Persistence of Evil*, 127.

28. Duane A. Priebe, "Mutual Fecundation: The Creative Interplay of Texts and New Contexts," in Karen L. Bloomquist, ed., and Lutheran World Federation, *Transformative Theological Perspectives* (Lutheran University Press, 2009), 91.

Conclusion: Creation, Context, and Connections

Despite interesting textual similarities with Hebrew Bible creation themes, the sea monster of Kwakwaka'wakw myth is not a creation motif. The sea monster is primarily a family crest, not an elemental figure of chaos. However, the parallels that do exist can tell us something about the human imagination and our "competing symbolic systems," which are "human attempts to live with divinity, and to transcend the specter of death."[29]

Studying and attempting to interpret the traditions of another culture raises profound questions of method, right, colonialism, appropriation, and hermeneutics in general. The foreign intricacies of the Kwakwaka'wakw culture should remind us that even those traditions we claim as our own are stranger, more profoundly *different*, than we may assume. We can so easily take Psalm 74 or Genesis 1 at surface value, assigning objective validity[30] based on our own limited experience, and forgetting that the cultural distance is even greater.

N. Clayton Croy points out that writing rather than reading is the proper activity of someone who insists on creating her own meaning.[31] Texts are always stranger, more complex, and more urgent than they appear on first reading. The best imaginative work will dig deeply, to try to understand. It then exegetes and combines meaning in new and compelling ways, imbuing ever more abundance into the living conversation between reader, text, and worldview. This "mutual fecundation"[32] finally means that the meaning of creation expands as we make more connections among sacred texts, that the truth of Christ which takes up the "whole of human culture" is expanding with the rest of the universe.

---

29. Michael Fishbane, *The Garments of Torah: Essays in Biblical Hermeneutics* (Indiana University Press, 1992), 131.

30. Rudolf Bultmann, "New Testament and Mythology," in Robert A. Segal, *Theories of Myth: Philosophy, Religious Studies, and Myth* (New York: Garland, 1996), 39.

31. N. Clayton Croy, *Prima Scriptura: An Introduction to New Testament Interpretation* (Grand Rapids, Mich.: Baker Academic, 2011), xxv.

32. Priebe in Bloomquist, "Transformative Theological Perspectives," 91.

And All the Tribes Fear Him

The creation of the world is as much metaphor as material. When we have satisfied our need for security and sustenance, we move on to poetry and making meaning. The monsters that beset us, the churning surf that rises at the edges of the unsuspected reef, come to represent the very chaos that stirs in the depths of our particular worlds.

The model totem pole that originally inspired this study featured a nursing mother as well as a sea monster. Like pregnancy, the sea monster rises out of unexpected depths in a swollen wash of salt water. The creation of the world and of a child are mysterious, fecund, rich processes that are gravid with fear and chaos, loss of control, threatened by powers at the limits of our being.

Part of the Christian claim about salvation is that God will redeem our sins of imagination as well as action; that every meaning will ultimately contribute to the Logos. God made this possible by emerging into the world through the watery womb of a human woman. Jesus connects the sign of Jonah with his own passion; in later Christian tradition, the routing of Hell is pictured as Christ overcoming a monster with a gaping maw. Thus is the new creation made possible. And thus Mary holding her child is one of the thrones of God, and she is seated in triumph on the ancient sea monster.

Appendix

Iceland, January 2010: A Mythic Meditation

> *I was studying abroad in Iceland on January 12, 2010, when a 7.0 magnitude earthquake in Haiti killed between 150,000 and 300,000 people, including my friend and fellow student, Benjamin Splichal Larson. I wrote this prose poem shortly after returning to Wartburg Theological Seminary. For more about the earthquake, read* A Witness: The Haiti Earthquake, a Song, Death, and Resurrection, *written by Renee Splichal Larson and edited by me. Renee was with Ben in Haiti and survived the earthquake, as did Ben's cousin Jonathan Larson.*

> So much depends upon
> the meaning we make. Every word
> has each its several senses,
> each its many myths, knotted and hung
> on each its teased and twisted yarn
> of combed and carded connotations,
> all stirred and animated by breath.

The shower water at home smells strange now, too sweet, like cedar and urine. I miss the strong smell of Icelandic hot water: Pure glacial runoff or ancient springwater, heated by the fires of the earth and perfumed with sulfur.

Iceland, January 2010: A Mythic Meditation

In Iowa I often walk up the great hall at New Melleray Abbey to receive a blessing. In Iceland I walked up the aisle of the cathedral at Skálholt to give a reading. The mural Christ loomed ahead, welcoming my awkward approach. My voice was low and trembling, hardly the bold minister of Christ's mystery that Paul's text proclaimed. "Although I am the very least of all the saints, this grace was given to me to bring to the Gentiles the news of the boundless riches of Christ, and to make everyone see what is the plan of the mystery hidden for ages in God who created all things." It was Epiphany, and it worked a change in me.

> My friend Ben Larson once said: "I don't think God fears our death the way we fear it. . . . I think maybe God mourns it."

Things I Saw in Iceland

I saw the drowning pool at Thingvellir.

I saw a troll at Selfoss.

I saw Athena towering over a hillside in a huge, dark cloud, and Arachne spinning, all a-tremble, at its base.

I saw our galaxy flung across the sky at Skálholt.

I saw the earth divided near Keflavik and at Thingvellir.

I saw a bäckahästen in a gully.

I saw a cemetery in Reykjavik.

I saw the volcano Hekla.

I saw a stone coffin and Snæfriður slipping
through the tunnel.

I saw a sea stack, a lighthouse, and a double rainbow.

I saw a horse with its rider at tölt.

I saw a dragon under the sand near the Blue Lagoon.

I saw Christ emerging from the colorscape, arms flung wide.

Appendices: Applied Mythology

The land is old, the history is old, but geologically it is newborn. At Thingvellir the moss is finger-deep or deeper, folded gently over the sharp volcanic terrain. Blue coins wink like stars at the bottom of frigid faults full of water.

Skálholt. Skyr. The mystery of Christ. The sky, the sun, the stars, the water. The food. The friends. The buildings and the glass and steel and concrete. The stones, rocks, boulders, ice, lava, mountains. The slender elf-body. The showers at the swimming hall—unaccustomed exposure. The blue lagoon. A hug, a kiss on the cheek. One Lord.

The shackles of postmodern perspective—that cold, dry voice that questions everything but answers nothing. The tears that are the wine of blessedness.[1] The tears that are the wine of sorrow. Life and death are in the cup. Our Lord drank it and we drink of it too, of Him too. Miskunna þú oss. Come, Lord Jesus. Have mercy. Lord, save.

When will our one Lord come? When will I be able to love my brothers and sisters in Christ as I am loved by Christ? When will anxiety and self-consciousness be replaced by perfect love?

> I feared when I read Colossians 3:3. When I knew Ben was dead, I began to hear *Heleluyan*,[2] from the liturgy he taught us. I heard *Heleluyan* for days, echoing in my ears, trembling on my lips, sounding in my throat. A friend helped me sing it. We left our tears on an Icelandic altar.

"We are only 300,000." The Icelanders are a people few in number but with the deepest roots, bound to the heart of the earth and swaying with the deepest seas. The map of Iceland in City Hall. The simple and clear boundaries of an island in the wide, wide sea. We seek a homeland. Iceland is a place of fire, ice, light, darkness,

---

1. "Their hearts, wounded with sweet words, overflowed, and their joy was like swords, and they passed in thought out to regions where pain and delight flow together and tears are the very wine of blessedness." —J.R.R. Tolkien, *The Lord of the Rings*, Book Six, Chapter 4.

2. Muscogee (Creek) Hallelujah Hymn. https://www.youtube.com/watch?v=WIwkzUZUMIk.

Iceland, January 2010: A Mythic Meditation

wool and fate, poetry and faith. Nature has done so much. The utter North.[3] I heard a voice crying, "Baldr the beautiful is dead, is dead!"[4] The Milky Way spread across the skies over Skálholt. The lights of the greenhouses at Selfoss. Water, water, water, light and sea and skies. The skull of Ymir, chaos yawned, the light separated from darkness and water from water. Grass was there nowhere, but then, the manes of the horses, the joy of the tölt. Óðinn with the ravens Huginn and Muninn, thought and memory, seated on eight-legged Sleipnir at a flying pace. The land is too young for clay. Little remains of the elder days but a stone coffin and the memories of the people, full of poetry, persistent as water. A long fire trough whose stones were laid in 871, a few years after Christ.

In summer, bumblebees and flowers, fjords and endless sunlight. But now, in winter, twilight on the clouds for hours and hours; piercing starlight, running water. The outlines of volcanoes, the manes of the horses. The strong smells and flavors of Icelandic food, the strong sensations and joys of Icelandic hospitality.

A language unchanged by the centuries, poetry still read in the original tongue. *Logos.*

A fierce people, the ravenous and bloodthirsty Vikings, now hungry for the bread that is Christ's body, thirsty for the cup that is his blood. *Mythos.*

> Fate, anxiety, mystery, faith.
>
> So much stress, and why?
> I cannot extend my life by taking thought.
>
> It's difficult to explain,
> but it goes a little something like this.
>
> God didn't save Ben. Why should I worry?

---

3. Reepicheep sought the utter East.
4. C.S. Lewis said, "I knew nothing about Baldr; but instantly I was uplifted into huge regions of northern sky, I desired with almost sickening intensity something never to be described."

Appendices: Applied Mythology

*The foolish man lies awake all night
and worries about things;
he's tired out when the morning comes
and everything's just as bad as it was.*

—The Poetic Edda

*The thing that I fear comes upon me,
and what I dread befalls me.
I am not at ease, nor am I quiet;
I have no rest; yet trouble comes.*

—Job 3:26

In Iceland I learned how to better talk to people I don't know. I learned a little about asking questions and listening to the answers. I learned to notice who was paying for my lobster and seek a conversation. In that way I found one of the few "ceramicists" (potters) in Iceland and received a picture of her work and a shy but excited explanation. (She imports her clay body from Holland. She lives near Skálholt.) I found out that my other table-mate spins yarn and makes sweaters.

When I was already familiar with a fairy-story, I learned to appreciate a new telling. The danger is when you are too eager to demonstrate how much you already know. But if you silence Anna Rún by explaining that Anna Margrét has already told the story of Thor and Loki among the Jotuns, and that Gunnar her father (who can lift 570 pounds) has interpreted it, you won't get to hear Anna Rún tell the tale in her sweet, strangely mature twelve-year-old way, a halting story from a girl who hasn't yet learned to enjoy putrefied shark meat but will examine, explain, and enjoy with you page after page of photos of the sublime sculpture of Einar Jónsson.

Wool and fate and spinning. I saw Athena glowering overhead as like Arachne I struggled with my puny art. Making new meaning, pulling the strands and twisting them into one, creating a cloak or a blanket or a sweater, a poem or a book or a psalm. And then cutting the thread, the cruel Norns. Imagine seeing those gnarled hands, hearing the wisdom of Urðr, feeling the numinous approach of Skuld, of Atropos who wields the shears. At her coming Hekla trembles and Haiti writhes, crushing my friend and countless poor and helpless people. *Les miserables* in Iceland and Haiti, in the arctic circle and on the equator. Iceland's Bell tolls for thee.

Iceland, January 2010: A Mythic Meditation

A living sacrifice. Be transformed by the renewing of your mind. How can I throw off postmodernism and put on Christ? Lord, have mercy. Drottinn, miskunna þú oss.

> Rings on our fingers, our ears pierced,[5]
> thralls and δουλοι of one Drottinn.

> Servants and slaves of one another.

Visit for a week and write a book; visit for a month and write an article; visit for a year and keep your mouth shut. Two weeks is just long enough for the gloss to lose a little luster, for us to absorb each other's delights and begin to perceive each other's sorrows, to glimpse the vices under the virtues. But our love may be all the deeper for that, because we are one in Christ our Savior, Redeemer, and Lord.

> Grammar and færie, λογος and magic.

> Pulling thoughts out of my head and onto the page,
> like spinning yarn.

A song from my childhood: *"Eli, eli, lama sabachthani! Abba, El Shaddai, to God I give my life."*

> *Heleluyan,* the great thanksgiving. One day I will hear
> *Heleluyan* again, herald for the coming of the Presence.
> *Heleluyan* will be our joyful response, led by our brother Ben.

---

5. Exodus 21:5–6.

Appendix

Advent

Silent night after silent night
we have waited in darkness for the coming of the Lord.

Like the fathomless sea is the night: heavy, dark waters above the sky. Gazing up, we peer down into eternal depths, waiting for the God of Heaven to come, to come and rescue us from darkness and from death.

A light shines in that darkness. And one comes.
One comes like a star from the boundless depths of the black ocean above, wrapped in clouds and thick darkness, yet glimmering with a light of breathless, insistent hope.

O Lord, your way is through the sea, your path, through the mighty waters; yet your footprints are unseen.

The Ancient of Days is wrought in darkness, in secret places, wonderfully and fearfully made in the mystery of God and the body of a young woman.

The LORD said to our Lord, from the womb of the morning like dew your youth shall come to you.

Advent

He who rides on the clouds, who utters his voice in thunder,
who stills the seas and made the stars,

The firstborn of all creation, before us but after us,
the bright and morning star, the divider of darkness,
is coming to save.

We wait with all the world.
With the ocean above and the one below,
with the clouds, the wind, with the skies and seas,
with every creature that breathes the breath of life
and holds that breath in hope

Until the coming of that one
and the atmospheric alleluia.

Appendix

Vigil

WE HAVE SEEN THE labor pains of creation. From the Spirit's swirling storm on the face of the abyss, to the burning light of the supernovas that forge every element; from the earthquakes and volcanoes that quicken our planet, to the crashing waters that draw us down into death.

Our God is the Living Word who calls into existence the things that are not and endows them with the joy and power and complexity of being. Nebula and neuron, quark and quasar, moon and mountain, snowflake and Serengeti, cherubim and chlorophyll: All that is, seen and unseen, known and unknowable.

This God loves and redeems all creation. This God says, Look, I am making everything new. This our God plucks us from the waters of chaos and sets us on the Living Rock.

The evening and the morning are the first day. After darkness and the silence of God in the death of Jesus Christ, a new day breaks and the shadows flee away. The light shines on a great mountain that fills the new earth. The light gleams green in the garden of God and blazes on the healing leaves of the tree of life. The first Word in the new creation is a voice that speaks our own name. And all the children of God will shout for joy.

—*Originally published on* Transpositions *(www.transpositions.co.uk).*

Appendix

Picture Perfect

"I need—no, I have the *right*—to be unlimited."

THIS CURIOUS CLAIM COMES from a Sprint commercial for the iPhone 5. The title: "I am unlimited: Picture Perfect."[1]

The commercial brilliantly captures a very noticeable movement with the rise of social media plus cheap memory plus cloud computing: As it becomes more and more possible to record and publish everything, it starts to feel more and more like an imperative. "We can share every second in data dressed as pixels. . . . Uploading the human experience." So why wouldn't we?

Finally, we have the ability to capture every precious second of this fleeting life. Thanks to my smartphone, my Facebook account, and a host of other technologies and media, I can capture and control my story in photos and status posts, crafting a tale that might fool even me into thinking my life is Picture Perfect. And because the Internet is forever, I can "upload all of me" into the immortal cloud. Nothing need be lost; nothing need truly die.

This is our classic sin dressed up in new, bit-based garb: idolatry. The Tower of Babel had nothing on social media for letting

---

1. Full transcript: *[Male Announcer] The miraculous is everywhere. In our homes, in our minds. We can share every second in data dressed as pixels. A billion roaming photojournalists . . . Uploading the human experience. And it is spectacular. So why would you cap that? My iPhone 5 can see every point of view, every panorama. The entire gallery of humanity. I need to upload all of me. I need, no, I have the right to be unlimited. Only Sprint offers Truly Unlimited data for iPhone 5.*

us clamber into the heavens and make an everlasting name for ourselves. To be unlimited, like gods.

Contrast this rosy picture with the biblical witness: Humanity is a "wind that passes and comes not again," like grass that grows up and then withers, "a mere breath." During Lent we are reminded that we are dust, and to dust we will return.[2]

And what about the cloud? This heavenly metaphor conceals the reality: that our cloud of immortal information is housed in relentlessly material and earthly banks of servers, gorging on electricity, in constant danger of overheating and continuously lavished with expensive air conditioning, attended by armies of analysts (highly skilled and well paid) who keep the precious data organized, integrated, and accessible. As the information swells, so do the resources it demands.

Because simply storing the data is not enough. As British logician Augustus de Morgan said in 1847: Nobody can rummage the library.[3] As we store every book, broadcast, and story, every tweet, every photo, every "like," every video, every Internet expression and transaction of fact, opinion, marketing, purchase, sale, and sentiment, we must simultaneously develop new, more comprehensive ways to search, curate, and filter the information. A virtual needle is lost in the Internet haystack if it is not indexed and findable by the person who wants it. This is what the information technology industry calls "big data" and information theory historian James Gleick calls "a flood."

And we do perceive it as a flood. When we are not exulting in the opportunity to "be unlimited" in the cloud, we are floundering frantically in a sea of data with a sensation of drowning. This is information overload.

Don't get me wrong: I love my smartphone, social media, and all the rest. As the Sprint commercial says, it is spectacular. But let's not imagine that we are unlimited. There is only one who knows

---

2. Psalms 39:5, 11; 78:39; 90:5–6; 103:14.

3. Quoted in James Gleick, "Drowning, surfing and surviving," *New Scientist* 210, no. 2806 (April 2, 2011): 30–31. See also Gleick's *The Information: A History, a Theory, a Flood* (Pantheon, 2011).

every sparrow and who both names and numbers every star; who lovingly notes the hairs on our heads, knows our every thought, and keeps our every tear. This one does not rely on any number of servers, nor require anything from us—not sacrifice, and certainly not electricity.[4]

Someday our machines will all shut down and our satellites will spin out of the skies. Anyone who really wishes to "upload all of me" must trust in a powerful creator who knows our every aspect and whose memory is eternal; who can make living beings out of dust; who can draw us out of the floods of death and set us on a living Rock. Who can finally remake us in the picture-perfect image of the only one who can truthfully say: "I am unlimited."

—*Originally published on* Transpositions *(www.transpositions.co.uk).*

[4]. Psalm 50:12–15.

Appendix

A Night at the Salt Kiln

Darkness, and a tall flame: the salt kiln at night. I am sitting in the warm summer evening with my friend Julia, the potter who is firing the kiln. We are on a farm in rural Iowa. The stars are brilliant, and there are fireflies, and the soft sounds of sheep over on the hill. A creek babbles to itself nearby, its banks littered with broken pots like old and cast-off gods. From the kiln comes the muffled roaring of a two-thousand-degree fire.

Pottery is an ancient and beautiful art, something we have been doing since God first formed our primeval parents from the dust of the earth. Pottery is the art of mud, something every child practices. It is the paragon of culture for archeologists; practically eternal unless it is broken or smashed. Yet it is a delicate art. When forming a bowl on the wheel, a potter must be mindful of every move, each application of pressure, any inadvertent jostle of her work. Clay takes in information as naturally as humans do, and holds onto it far longer. A bumped pot likely means a warped one after the firing.

The salt kiln is a large, permanent structure somewhat like a haystack in size and shape. It is made of bricks and adobe, and sheltered by an A-frame roof with wooden rafters, pierced by the tall chimney. The kiln is fired by hand in a process that consumes three days and nights and cords of high-quality firewood. Inside is the hopeful work of several potters: bowls, cups, sculpture. Some of it will be ruined in the process; some of it will emerge in unexpected and colorful glory.

We are waiting for the right moment, sometime in the early hours of the morning, when the kiln will reach 2,275 degrees. Already when we remove a brick to peep inside, the pottery is white-hot and we must wear protective goggles against the black-body radiation. When the kiln reaches temperature, we will throw pounds of salt in the door, then retreat until the toxic fumes subside. The salt will fuse with the ash and the chemical glazes on the pots to create crystals, colors, texture, and other surprises.

But for now there is only the dark of the night and the heat of the fire. For me, the spiritual atmosphere is almost as charged as the kiln. As fire comes spurting out of its tall chimney, the flames tinged with green and purple as the chemicals within combine, I think of King Nebuchadnezzar's burning fiery furnace that was made seven times hotter—surely no hotter than this furnace. I think of the dark night of the soul, when God forms and shapes us in our despair and misery. I think of Adam and Eve, formed of clay. I think of myself, seeking to make and to be art, to take in information and to shape it, to be conformed to the image of Christ and be transformed by the renewing of my mind. A living sacrifice. I think of the disciples of Christ and the salt of the earth. "Everyone will be salted with fire." "Our God is a consuming fire."

Now it is midnight; the fireflies have gone in, but the stars still watch. Julia and I hover in the dark, pushing more wood into the fiery door every few minutes, watching the chimney flames compete with the moon for brightness. The farmer who owns this land stops by; we talk about the nearby sheep. He tells us a story about shepherding. "I never use my voice when I want the sheep to move along ahead of me," he says. "I wave a plastic bag on a stick, and it alarms them enough that they start walking. But I never use my voice harshly from behind them. I only call them from ahead. This way they continue to love and trust my voice, and come willingly when I call."

A plastic bag on a stick; a wisp of white in the dark. Christ is the good shepherd as well as God the consuming fire. There is darkness, and clay, and pressure, and flame; but there is also the voice of Jesus, sounding in the night, leading us through the valley of the shadow of death and on into the morning. With God, creation and redemption and judgment are all one mighty act of love. Christ is the good shepherd who came to seek and save, who loves us to death—his death and ours. This is the God who fires a handful of clay to make living art.

The kiln hit temperature around three in the morning. We salted it three times, then went home. Three days later, the kiln was opened and Julia gave me the cup I had made. It is pitted and textured, blue and brown and white and gray, rough and smooth, glossy and matte. It is beautiful. It is transformed.

Bibliography

Armstrong, Karen. *A History of God: The 4,000-Year Quest of Judaism, Christianity and Islam*. New York: Random House, 1997.
Athanasius. *On the Incarnation: De Incarnatione Verbi Dei*. Crestwood, NY: St Vladimir's Seminary Press, 1996.
Augustine. *The Literal Meaning of Genesis: De Genesi Ad Litteram*. Translated and annotated by John Hammond Taylor, S.J. Ancient Christian Writers 41:1. New York: Paulist, 1982.
Barthes, Roland. *Mythologies*. New York: Farrar, Straus and Giroux, 1972.
Bauer, Walter. *A Greek-English Lexicon of the New Testament and Other Early Christian Literature*. Edited by Frederick William Danker. Chicago: University of Chicago Press, 2001.
Becker, Ernest. *The Denial of Death*. New York: Free Press, 1997.
Brown, Francis, S. R. Driver, and Charles A. Briggs. *Brown-Driver-Briggs Hebrew and English Lexicon*. Peabody, MA: Hendrickson, 1996.
Bultmann, Rudolf. *Kerygma and Myth*. Edited by Hans Werner Bartsch. New York: Harper & Row, 1961.
Cahill, Thomas. *Desire of the Everlasting Hills: The World Before and After Jesus*. New York: Anchor, 2001.
Campbell, Joseph. *The Hero with a Thousand Faces*. Novato, CA: New World Library, 2008.
———. *The Inner Reaches of Outer Space: Metaphor as Myth and as Religion*. Novato, CA: New World Library, 2002.
Charbonneau-Lassay, Louis. *The Bestiary of Christ*. Translated by D.M. Dooling. Arkana, NY: Penguin, 1992.
Childs, Brevard S. *Myth and Reality in the Old Testament*. Studies in Biblical Theology 27. First Series. Naperville, IL: A.R. Allenson, 1960.
Collins, John J. *Introduction to the Hebrew Bible*. Minneapolis: Augsburg Fortress, 2004.
Crossley-Holland, Kevin. *The Norse Myths*. New York: Pantheon, 1981.

Bibliography

Doty, William G. "Mythophiles' Dyscrasia: A Comprehensive Definition of Myth." *Journal of the American Academy of Religion* 48 (December 1980) 531–61.

Fishbane, Michael. *Biblical Myth and Rabbinic Mythmaking*. New York: Oxford University Press, 2005.

———. *The Garments of Torah: Essays in Biblical Hermeneutics*. Indiana University Press, 1992.

Giere, Samuel D. *A New Glimpse of Day One: Intertextuality, History of Interpretation, and Genesis 1.1–5*. New York: De Gruyter, 2010.

———. "'This Is My World!' Son of Man (Jezile) and Cross-Cultural Convergences of Bible and World." In *Son of Man: An African Jesus Film*, edited by Richard Walsh, Jeffery L. Staley, and Adele Reinhartz, 23–33. The Bible in the Modern World 52. Sheffield: Sheffield Phoenix, 2013.

Gleick, James. "How Information Became a Thing, and All Things Became Information." DiscoverMagazine.com, September 14, 2011. http://discovermagazine.com/2011/jul-aug/09-how-information-became-a-thing.

———. "What We Don't Know: Is the Universe Actually Made of Information?" Wired.com, February 1, 2007. http://www.wired.com/wired/archive/15.02/bigquestions.html.

Graves, Robert. *The White Goddess*. New York: Farrar, Straus and Giroux, 1981.

Greene, Brian. *The Fabric of the Cosmos: Space, Time, and the Texture of Reality*. New York: Vintage Books, 2005.

Guite, Malcolm. *Faith, Hope and Poetry: Theology and the Poetic Imagination*. Great Britain: Ashgate, 2012.

Gustafson, Scott W. *Evil and the Followers of Jesus: Theodicy as Foundation for Christian Ethics*. Great Falls, VA: Bradwell Books, 1996.

Hart, Trevor A., and Steven R. Guthrie, eds. *Faithful Performances*. Burlington, VT: Ashgate, 2007.

Hough, Andrew. "Stephen Hawking: 'Heaven Is a Fairy Story for People Afraid of the Dark.'" *The Telegraph*, May 16, 2011.

James, William. *The Will to Believe and Other Essays in Popular Philosophy, and Human Immortality*. New York: Dover, 1960.

Jeffrey Johnson, Kirstin Elizabeth. "Rooted in All Its Story, More Is Meant than Meets the Ear: A Study of the Relational and Revelational Nature of George MacDonald's Mythopoeic Art." PhD diss., University of St Andrews, 2011. http://research-repository.st-andrews.ac.uk/handle/10023/1887.

Jenson, Robert W. *Ezekiel*. Grand Rapids, MI: Brazos, 2009.

———. *On Thinking the Human*. Grand Rapids: Eerdmans, 2003.

John Paul II. *Man and Woman He Created Them: A Theology of the Body*. Boston, MA: Pauline Books & Media, 2006.

Jüngel, Eberhard. *God as the Mystery of the World: On the Foundation of the Theology of the Crucified One in the Dispute Between Theism and Atheism*. Grand Rapids: Eerdmans, 1983.

BIBLIOGRAPHY

Kelley, Melissa M. *Grief: Contemporary Theory and the Practice of Ministry*. Minneapolis: Fortress, 2010.

Kolb, Robert, Timothy Wengert, and James Schaffer. *The Book of Concord: The Confessions of the Evangelical Lutheran Church*. Minneapolis: Fortress, 2001.

Kruglinski, Susan. "What Makes You Uniquely 'You'?" DiscoverMagazine.com, January 16, 2009. http://discovermagazine.com/2009/feb/16-what-makes-you-uniquely-you.

Levenson, Jon D. *The Death and Resurrection of the Beloved Son: The Transformation of Child Sacrifice in Judaism and Christianity*. New Haven: Yale University Press, 1993.

———. *Sinai and Zion: An Entry into the Jewish Bible*. New York: HarperOne, 1987.

Lewis, C.S. *The Great Divorce*. New York: Macmillan, 1978.

———. *The Problem of Pain*. New York: Macmillan, 1962.

———. *Studies in Medieval and Renaissance Literature*. Cambridge: University Press, 1966.

Lightman, Alan P. "The Accidental Universe: Science's Crisis of Faith." Harpers.org, December 2011. http://harpers.org/archive/2011/12/0083720.

Luther, Martin. *Luther's Works*. Edited by Jaroslav Pelikan and Walter A. Hansen. Vol. 27. Saint Louis, MO: Concordia Publishing House, 1964.

MacDonald, George. *The Imagination, and Other Essays*. Boston: D. Lothrop and Company, 1883.

Mannermaa, Tuomo. *Christ Present in Faith: Luther's View of Justification*. Minneapolis: Fortress, 2005.

McAdams, Dan P. *The Stories We Live By: Personal Myths and the Making of the Self*. New York: Guilford, 1997.

McDermott, Gerald. "Evangelicals Divided." *First Things*, April 2011. http://www.firstthings.com/article/2011/04/evangelicals-divided.

O'Flaherty, Wendy Doniger. "Inside and Outside the Mouth of God: The Boundary between Myth and Reality." In *Theories of Myth*, edited by Robert A. Segal, 279–311. Philosophy, Religious Studies, and Myth 3. New York: Garland, 1996.

Origen. *Origen On First Principles: Being Koetschau's Text of the De Principiis Translated into English, Together with an Introduction and Notes by G.W. Butterworth*. Translated by G. W. Butterworth. Gloucester, MA: Peter Smith, 1973.

Polkinghorne, John. *Faith of a Physicist*. Minneapolis: Augsburg Fortress, 1996.

Rae, Murray. *History and Hermeneutics*. London: T&T Clark, 2006.

Ricoeur, Paul. *Interpretation Theory: Discourse and the Surplus of Meaning*. Fort Worth, TX: Texas Christian University Press, 1976.

———. *The Symbolism of Evil*. Religious Perspectives 17. New York: New York, Harper & Row, 1967.

Bibliography

Robinson, Marilynne. "The Book of Books: What Literature Owes the Bible." NYTimes.com, December 22, 2011. http://www.nytimes.com/2011/12/25/books/review/the-book-of-books-what-literature-owes-the-bible.html.

Schaff, Philip, ed. *Nicene and Post-Nicene Fathers* 7. First Series. New York: The Christian Literature Company, 1888.

———. *Nicene and Post-Nicene Fathers* 7. Second Series. New York: The Christian Literature Company, 1888.

Segal, Robert A., ed. *Theories of Myth: From Ancient Israel and Greece to Freud, Jung, Campbell, and Lévi-Strauss.* Philosophy, Religious Studies, and Myth 3. New York: Garland, 1996.

Smith, Christian, and Patricia Snell. *Souls in Transition: The Religious and Spiritual Lives of Emerging Adults.* New York: Oxford University Press, 2009.

Splichal Larson, Renee. *A Witness: The Haiti Earthquake, a Song, Death, and Resurrection.* Eugene, OR: Wipf and Stock, 2016.

Tillich, Paul. *Dynamics of Faith.* New York: Harper & Brothers, 1958.

———. *Systematic Theology* 1. Chicago: University of Chicago Press, 1973.

Tolkien, J.R.R. *Tree and Leaf.* London: HarperCollins, 2001.

Toolan, David. "Praying in a Post-Einsteinian Universe." *Cross Currents* 46 (Winter 1996) 437–70.

Tracy, David. *Plurality and Ambiguity: Hermeneutics, Religion, Hope.* Chicago: University of Chicago Press, 1994.

UBS Greek New Testament: A Reader's Edition. Stuttgart: Deutsche Bibelgesellschaft and United Bible Societies, 2007.

Vivas, Eliseo. "Myth: Some Philosophical Problems." In *Theories of Myth*, edited by Robert A. Segal, 341–55. Philosophy, Religious Studies, and Myth 3. New York: Garland, 1996.

Ward, Michael. *Planet Narnia: The Seven Heavens in the Imagination of C.S. Lewis.* New York: Oxford University Press, 2008.

Yarchin, William. *History of Biblical Interpretation: A Reader.* Peabody, MA: Baker Academic, 2004.

Subject Index

Anselm, 15
apologetics, 1, 14, 44, 44n26
Armstrong, Karen, 30, 30n40
Artemis of Ephesus, 69
Athanasius, 12, 12n18, 22, 27n31, 47, 78n36, 88n80
Atrahasis, 38n6, 61n43
Augustine, 26n26, 38
Avis, Paul, 15n26

Barfield, Owen, 79
Barthes, Roland, 9n6
Bauer, Walter, 5n9, 62n47
Becker, Ernest, 21–22, 24–26, 28–29, 53, 71, 84
biblical myth, 12, 33n53, 38n6, 61n43
Book of Nature, 65, 70
breath (see also *vanity, wind*), 26n28, 29, 46, 47, 50, 50n47, 63, 68, 102, 108, 109, 112
Bultmann, Rudolf, 9, 10, 12, 12n17, 24, 24n19, 26n25, 31, 38–39, 41, 83, 100n30

Cahill, Thomas, 3n2
Campbell, Joseph, 16–17, 73n23
Charbonneau-Lassay, Louis, 61n45
Childs, Brevard, 77

Colbert, Stephen, 76n29
Collins, John, 36n1, 61n43
crisis, 83

doom, 83–84
Doty, William, 8n3

elemental spirits, 73n23
Eliade, Mircea, 7
Eliot, George, 66n62
Enuma Elish, 38n6, 61n43, 97, 99
Eros and Psyche, 70
eucatastrophe, 40n13
evil, 49, 50, 56n23, 67, 86, 99
exegesis, 56–58, 60, 62, 78, 81, 82, 86
exegete, exegetical, 10, 14, 16, 18, 56–61, 61n43, 62, 66–68, 81, 85, 87, 100

failure of imagination, 17, 48, 55, 74, 87, 88
Fishbane, Michael, 8, 9n4, 10–14, 16–17, 20, 28, 37, 38, 38n6, 42–44, 56–64, 66, 71, 77, 100n29
Flight from Death, 21n6
fundamentalism, 12, 14, 44

Subject Index

Gadamer, Hans Georg, 78
Giere, Samuel, xi, 64n53, 64n55, 79n43
Gleick, James, 5n10, 5n12, 112
graven images, 42, 43
Graves, Robert, 37
Greene, Brian, 32
Gregory of Nazianzus, 34n57
Guite, Malcolm, 5n11, 15n26
Gustafson, Scott, 50n45

Hart and Guthrie, 82n54
Hawking, Stephen, 27
Hegel, 84n66
Heidegger, 84n66
hermeneutics, 1, 15, 40, 100
hero, heroes, 16, 26, 28–30, 36, 37, 49, 53, 55, 66, 83, 84, 86
Holm, Bill, xi, 93–94

idolatry, idols, 4n5, 12n18, 17, 25, 26, 27n31, 28, 29, 34, 45–48, 69, 71, 72, 74, 76, 76n30, 86, 87, 90, 111
informed substance, 31–32, 34, 78
inspiration, 15, 20, 40, 43, 57, 60n40, 63–66, 78, 86, 101
intertextuality, 79, 80
Israel, 14, 32, 43n23, 45n29, 58, 71, 94, 98–99

Jacob, 32, 42
James, William, 30, 32n46, 53, 54
Jeffrey Johnson, Kirstin, xi, 37, 40–41, 59–60, 60n40, 68n68, 68n70, 70, 78–82
Jenson, Robert, 22–24, 43n23
John Paul II, 4n6
Jüngel, Eberhard, vi, 25, 85n67

Kelley, Melissa, 4n7, 19n3, 54–55
Kruglinski, Susan, 7n16, 79n44

L'Engle, Madeleine, 20, 58–59

Levenson, Jon, 13–14, 42, 55n14, 68, 97, 99
Lewis, C.S., 2, 15n27, 23, 58, 60, 60n39, 61n45, 67, 68, 70–71, 73n21, 73n22, 75, 79, 80n47, 88n79, 105n3, 105n4
Lightman, Alan, 6n14
liturgy, 60n40, 81, 98, 99, 104
live wire, 30–31, 53, 62
logos, 5, 7, 11, 38, 62, 81, 88, 101, 105
Luther, Martin, 41n19, 45n28, 77n32, 86n71, 87n73
LXX, 5n8, 49, 49n42

MacDonald, George, vii, 37, 39–41, 58–60, 63n50, 68–70, 78–81, 88, 90
Mannermaa, Tuomo, 41n19, 82n58, 83n62, 83n63
materialist myth, 23, 24, 75–76, 83, 88
McAdams, Dan, 4n7, 52–56, 62, 87
McDermott, Gerald, 3n3
medieval, 56, 61n45, 67, 70
Melanchthon, 35n62
metaphor, 10–11, 11n14, 14, 43, 68, 92, 101, 112
Midrash, 56–58, 61n43
mortality salience, 21n6, 24, 26
Mudede, Charles, xi, 80n45
myth, definitions, 5, 8–9, 13, 16–17, 28, 87
myth theory, 8–9, 16, 31
mythology, Babylonian, 38n6, 61n43, 97
mythology, Canaanite, 11
mythology, Christian, 2, 70, 89
mythology, Greek, 2, 8, 10, 12n18, 32, 36, 69, 70–71, 103, 106
mythology, Norse, 2, 8, 36, 67, 70, 105–106
mythos, 5, 7, 11, 38, 39, 62, 88, 105

Subject Index

natural theology, 65
Nietzsche, 84n66

O'Flaherty, Wendy, 8n2, 60n40
Olson, Dan, xi, 53, 83, 85
Origen, 26n27, 63–64
Otto, Rudolf, 59n35
ouroboros, 61n45

Pascal's Wager, 23
Paul (apostle), 24, 45, 69, 70, 74, 103
physics, 2, 5–6, 6n13, 32, 75
Plato, 4, 6, 10–11, 55n19
Plymouth Brethren, 1
poetry, 5, 7, 37–38, 67, 87, 101, 105
Polkinghorne, John, 23
positivism, 4n6, 9, 10, 14, 14n25, 15, 25, 27, 31, 33, 36, 44n26, 75, 88
postmodernism, 4n6, 15, 25, 75, 87, 104, 107
Priebe, Duane, xi, 78n39, 80n45, 91, 94, 99, 100n32
principle of charity, 11, 38, 59
principle of parsimony, 11
principle of particularity, 17, 66, 80

Rae, Murray, 76
revelation, 43, 59, 60, 63n52, 81
Ricoeur, Paul, 11n14, 15, 64, 77n33, 78
Robinson, Marilynne, 32n50

sacramental worldview, 15, 38, 80, 80n47, 81
science, 2, 3, 5, 7, 33, 36n2, 65, 66, 75, 87
science and poetry, 5, 7, 87
Segal, Robert, 8, 12
Sisyphus, 32
Smith and Snell, 76n29

Splichal Larson, Renee, xi, 50n45, 102
sub-creation, 40, 59
symbols, 9, 15, 30–31, 39, 40, 53, 54, 60, 71, 80n47, 81, 100
systematic theology, 2, 3, 5, 15, 17, 91

thesaurus (see also *treasure*), 56, 57
Tillich, Paul, 3n4, 18n33, 22, 27, 30–31, 37, 39, 47n32, 50, 54, 76n30, 81n53, 87n72
Tolkien, J.R.R., 2, 40, 40n13, 58–59, 68, 70, 79, 82n56, 104n1
Toolan, David, 24n15
Tracy, David, 20, 33, 63, 66, 68
transference, 28
treasure (see also *thesaurus*), vi, 53, 56, 56n33, 68, 71

ultimate concern, 18, 18n33, 21, 22, 27, 27n31, 28, 47, 51, 54, 55, 58, 62, 76, 84, 87

vanity (see also *breath, wind*), 25, 50
verbal iconograph, 37
visible word, 38
Vivas, Eliseo, 7n17, 7n18, 19, 31–33, 38, 52, 81

Ward, Michael, 60n39, 71n9, 73n22, 80n47
Wartburg Theological Seminary, xi, 2, 53, 91, 102
Weltanschauung, 31, 80
what is assumed, 34, 34n57, 83, 85, 88
wind (see also *breath, vanity*), 20, 50, 67n65, 97, 109, 112
worldview, 9, 11, 31, 55, 76, 80, 83, 97, 100

Scripture Index

Genesis	7, 26n26, 33n53, 39	**Job**	97
		3:26	106
1	25, 57, 97, 100	26:12	49n41, 65n58
1–2	61n43	41:31–33, 10	95
1:2 (LXX)	5n8, 49		
1:4	33n53	**Psalms**	
1:26a	44	16:8–9	43
2:7	50n47	17:8	43
4:3–5	67	17:15	42n20
6:5	49	18	44
32:28	32n49	22:9	43
50:20	67n67	27:4, 8	42
		33:10–11	51
Exodus		39	22
21:5–6	107n5	39:5, 11	112n2
31:4	49n43	42:2	42
32:4	45n29	49:7–15	46
		50:12a	26
2 Samuel		50:12b	26n28
14:14	51	50:12–15	113
		63:8	43
1 Chronicles		71:6	43
28:9b	51	73:23	43
		74	43, 100
		74:12–17	97
		78:39	112n2
		90	22
		90:5	112n2

Scripture Index

Psalms (continued)

94:11	50
96:5	72n18
103:2–4	51
103:14	112n2
104	61n43, 97
106:20	45
115:4–9	46
119:97	65n56
135:15–18	46
136:5	49n41, 65n58
146:3–6	29
148	97

Proverbs

3:19	49n41, 65n58
19:21	50

Ecclesiastes 22, 25

9:1	83n59

Isaiah 44

2:1–4	71
26:19	89
40:28	49n41, 65n58
41:13	43
45:18	65n59
46	46n30
46:4	26
46:4b	35n60
59:7	50

Jeremiah

10:12	49n41, 65n58
29:11	51
31:33–34	77
51:15	49n41, 65n58

Lamentations

2:3b	58

Ezekiel 44

37:12	43n23

Jonah 101

1:17	96
2:8	48n35
2:10	96

Micah

4:5	71

Habakkuk

2:14	34, 88n75

Matthew

6:23	48n36
12:35	56n23
13:52	vi, 56n23, 71n10
22:20	vi, 37, 76

Mark

9:49	115

Luke

6:45	56n23

John

1:5	4n5
1:14, 16	49n38
1:18	vii, 41, 62
5:17	78n38
5:39–40	65n57
12:24–25	73n20
16:13	86n69

Scripture Index

Acts
17:16–33	69n2
17:24–25	26n28
19:34	69n1

Romans
1:4	85n68
1:20	5n8, 41, 64, 65n61, 70n5
1:22–23	45
3:23	48n37
4:17	28n35, 47n33
5:6	51n49
6:5	82n57, 88n82
6:21	73n19
8:29	48
12:1	83n60, 115
12:1–2	115

1 Corinthians
3:11–15	74
7:32ff	24n16
8:6	34n58
13:12	89n83
15:49	48

2 Corinthians
1:20	33n54
3:18	48
4:4	48
4:6	49n39
4:18	63
5:14	88n76
5:18–19, 14, 15	72n14
10:5b	88n78

Galatians
3:3	24n19
4:3, 9	73n23
4:9	73n23

Ephesians
1:4	78n37
1:23	72n16
2:21–22	73n24
3:8–9	103
3:19	50n44
4:8	88n77

Philippians
2:5–11	84
2:9–11	85n68
3:4ff	24n19

Colossians
1:15	42, 47, 61n44
1:15–16	5n8, 5n9
1:15–20	85
1:20	72n15
2:8	73n23
2:17	67n66
3:3	104
3:5–17	86
3:10	48
3:16a	85

2 Thessalonians
2:10b	35n61, 88n81

1 Timothy
1:4	73n25
1:17	41
4:7	73n25
6:16	41

2 Timothy
3:16	63n51
4:4	73n25

Titus

1:14	73n25

Hebrews

2:15	22
10:25	81n51
11:3	5n8
11:27	42, 86n70
12:29	115

James

1:14–15	50n46

1 Peter

3:15	44n26

2 Peter

1:16	73n25
3:10	73n23

1 John

3:2	48
4:12	41

Revelation

	39
21:26–27	72n17

www.ingramcontent.com/pod-product-compliance
Lightning Source LLC
Chambersburg PA
CBHW071443160426
43195CB00013B/2021